Alex Everett Frye

Brooks and Brook Basins

Alex Everett Frye
Brooks and Brook Basins
ISBN/EAN: 9783744661690

Printed in Europe, USA, Canada, Australia, Japan

Cover: Foto ©Thomas Meinert / pixelio.de

More available books at **www.hansebooks.com**

THE ROMANCE OF ZION CHAPEL

BY

RICHARD LE GALLIENNE

JOHN LANE: THE BODLEY HEAD
LONDON AND NEW YORK
1898

Contents

CHAPTER		PAGE
I	OF A CURIOUS MEETING OF EXTREMES	1
II	INTRODUCES MORE UNROMANTIC MATERIAL	5
III	OF ELI MOGGRIDGE AND THE NEW SPIRIT	11
IV	ENDS QUITE ROMANTICALLY	15
V	OF THE ARTIST IN MAN AND HIS MATERIALS	22
VI	OF A WONDERFUL QUALITY IN WOMEN	30
VII	THE LITERARY AND PHILOSOPHICAL SOCIETY OF COALCHESTER	38
VIII	THE PLOT AGAINST COALCHESTER	47
IX	"THE DAWN"	53
X	HOW THEY BROUGHT THE GOOD NEWS OF A MORRIS WALL-PAPER TO COALCHESTER	59
XI	A LITTLE ABOUT JENNY	66
XII	HOW THE RENAISSANCE CAME IN PERSON TO NEW ZION	70

CONTENTS

CHAPTER		PAGE
XIII	IN WHICH JENNY KISSES MR. MOGGRIDGE	99
XIV	THE GREAT EVENT OF MR. TALBOT'S LIFE	107
XV	JENNY'S BOTTOM DRAWER	113
XVI	THEOPHIL ALL THIS TIME	119
XVII	"O THAT 'T WERE POSSIBLE . . ."	130
XVIII	ONE DAY OUT OF ALL THE YEARS	135
XIX	PREPARATIONS FOR A FAST AND OTHER SADNESS	145
XX	IN WHICH JENNY CRIES	162
XXI	IN WHICH JENNY IS MYSTERIOUSLY HONOURED	173
XXII	THE TRYST LETHEAN	195
XXIII	JENNY'S LYING IN STATE	206
XXIV	THE BEGINNING OF THE PILGRIMAGE — A MESSAGE FROM JENNY	218
XXV	JENNY'S POSTE RESTANTE	233
XXVI	FURTHER CONCERNING THEOPHIL'S LIFE AFTER THE DEATH OF JENNY	237
XXVII	ISABEL CALLING	258
XXVIII	BACK IN ZION PLACE	270
XXIX	AND SUDDENLY THE LAST	281

The Romance of Zion Chapel

CHAPTER I

OF A CURIOUS MEETING OF EXTREMES

ON the dreary suburban edge of a very old, very ignorant, very sooty, hard-hearted, stony-streeted, meanly grim, little provincial town there stands a gasometer. On one side of this gasometer begins a region of disappointed fields, which, however, has hardly begun before a railway embankment cuts across, at an angle convenient for its entirely obscuring the few meadows and trees that in this desolate land do duty for a countryside. The dull workmen's streets that here abruptly present unfinished ends to the universe must console themselves with the gasometer. And indeed they seem more than content. For a street boasting the best view, as it runs out its sordid line longer than the rest, is proudly called Gasometer Street. Some of the streets that are denied the gasometer cluster narrow and dark, hardly built twenty years perhaps, yet long since drearily old, — with the unattractive antiquity of old iron and old clothes, — round a mouldy little chapel, in what we can only describe as the Wesleyan Methodist style of architecture. Cased in weather-stained and decaying stucco, it bears upon its front the words "New Zion," and the streets about it are named accordingly: Zion Passage, Zion Alley, Zion Walk, Zion Street. There is a house too which had been lucky enough to call itself Zion View, the very morning before the house at the corner had contemplated doing the same.

At Zion View lived and still lives Mr. Moggridge, the huge, good-natured, guffawing pillar of New Zion, — on whom, at the moment, however, we will not call.

A nice dull place, you may say, from which to issue invitations to a romance. Well, of course, it must seem so if pretty places are the reader's idea of romance. Curiously enough, the preference of the Lady Romance herself is for just such dull places. These dreary, soot-begrimed streets are the very streets she loves best to appear in, on a sudden, some astonished day, with a sound of silk skirts and a spring wind of attar of roses. Contrast, surprise, — these are her very soul. Dull places and bright people,— these she loves to bring together, and watch for laughter and tears. You are never safe from Romance, and the place to seek her is never the place where she was last found.

Well, at all events, it is to Gasometer Street and New Zion that you are respectfully invited, and before you decline the invitation with a shrug, I will tell you this about the gasometer. The romantic eyes of one of the greatest French poets once looked on that gasometer! I won't pretend that they dwelt there, but look on it they once did — the eyes of that great, sad, scandalous, religious French poet — on a night of weary rain that set someone quoting, — also in that street, —

> "Il pleure dans mon cœur
> Comme il pleut sur la ville."

Yes, and that French poet passed the gasometer on his way to New Zion. Actually.

Romance! Why, I wouldn't exchange Gasometer Street for the Isles of Greece!

CHAPTER II

INTRODUCES MORE UNROMANTIC MATERIAL

THAT French poet only concerns us here as, so to say, the highest light in the contrast which it was the happy business of Theophilus Londonderry, Jenny Talbot, and two or three devoted friends to make in the vicinity of Gasometer Street and indeed in little Coalchester at large.

Theophilus Londonderry! It is rather a mouthful of a name. Yet it's so like the long, expansive, good-natured, eloquent fellow it stands for, that I must not shorten it, though we shall presently abbreviate it for purposes of affectionate reference. He himself liked "Theophil" for its reminiscence of another French poet, though "Theo" was perhaps the more suitable abbreviation for one of his profession. Really, or perhaps rather seemingly, Theophilus Londonderry had two professions, — or say one was a profession and the other was a vocation, a "call." By day he professed to be a clerk in a cotton-office, — and he was no fool at that (there is no need for a clever man to be a fool at anything), but by night, and occasionally of an afternoon,— when he got leave of absence to solemnise a marriage, or run through a funeral, — he was a spiritual pastor, the young father of his flock.

Here I must permit myself some necessary remarks on the subject of Nonconformity, its influence on individualities and its direct relationship to Romance. In the churches of England or of Rome, — though he sometimes looked wistfully towards the latter, — Theophilus Londonderry, with his disabilities of worldly condition, would have found no place to be himself in. His was an organism that could not long have breathed in any rigid organisation. It was the non-establishment, the comparative free-field, of Nonconformity that gave him his chance. Conscious, soon after his first few breaths, of a personal force that claimed operation in some human employment, some work not made with hands, but into which also entered the spirit of man, and being quite poor, and entirely hopeless of family wealth or influence, there were only two fields open to him, Art or Nonconformity. To art in the usual sense of the word he was not called, but to the art of Demosthenes he was unmistakably called ; and for this Nonconformity — with a side entrance into politics — was his opportunity.

This bourne of his faculties had indeed been predestined for him by no remoter influence than his father, himself a lay-preacher, when he was not the business manager of a large hardware store, — a lay-preacher with a very gentle face, the face of a father, a woman, a saint, and a failure all in one.

I say failure by no means unkindly. Londonderry's father was made to be a good bishop, to radiate from a hallowed security sweet lights of blessing. His talent was gentleness, not in itself a fighting quality, — a quality that needs a place prepared for it, needs the hand of strength or opportunity to set it upon the hill. That he had made himself learned, that his sympathy knew much of the soul of man, that he was conscious of a very near communion with the Divine — were qualifications that alone might not avail. Yet were they not lost, for, apart from their own restricted exercise in the circle of his own little "cause" and the other causes for which, in the technical phrase, he would occasionally "supply," they had passed into his son, and met in him other more energetic qualities, such as a magnetic eloquence, a love of laughter, and a mighty humanity.

Thus Theophilus Londonderry was partly his father licked into shape and partly something bigger and more effectively vital.

At sixteen he was learned in all the theologies; at nineteen he was said to have preached a great sermon; at twenty-two he was the success of a big political meeting; and at twenty-four he was the new lay-pastor at New Zion.

This is not to be the theological history of a soul, so I shall not attempt to decide upon the exact proportion of literal acceptance of Christian dogma underlying the young pastor's sermons. I doubt if he could have told you himself, and I am sure he would have considered the point as unimportant as I do. His was a message of humanity delivered in terms of Christianity. The message was good, the meaning honest. He would, no doubt, have preferred another pulpit with other formulas, but that pulpit was not forthcoming; so, like all the strong and the wise, he chose the formulas offered to him, using as few as possible, and humanising all he used; and never for a single second of time, whatever the apparent contradictions on the surface, was Theophilus Londonderry that poorest of all God's creatures, — a hypocrite. However you may judge him, you must never make that mistake about him.

CHAPTER III

OF ELI MOGGRIDGE AND THE NEW SPIRIT

NEW ZION, despite its name, was, as I have hinted, no longer new. The fiery zeal which had once made it a living schism had long since died out of it. Carried years before, a little blazing ember of faith, from a flourishing hearth of Nonconformity some streets away, it had puffed and gleamed a little space in the eloquence of the offended zealots who carried it hotfoot that Sunday morning, but its central fire had been poor, and for a long time no evangelistic bellows had awakened in it even a spark.

Its original elders had long since lost heart and passed away. A dwindling remnant of their children, from old association, just kept its doors from actually closing, and made a mournful interruption in its musty silence on Sundays. Life was too low to support a Wednesday prayer-meeting, and Sunday by Sunday that life ebbed lower. New life from the outside must come, and speedily, or it must die.

But new life was already on the way. On the town side the sad streets round New Zion led one into a more prosperous High Street, and indeed Zion Street itself, as it turned the corner, flamed into quite a jovial and ruddy shop — a provision merchant's, and kept by Eli Moggridge. The name did its owner considerable wrong, for its suggestion of puritanical sanctimoniousness was a flat contradiction of the jovial and ruddy personality, the huge red-whiskered laugher, for whom it stood, and of whom the shop, with its healthy smell of cheese and its air of exuberant prosperity, was a much more truthful expression. Well, the business was growing with such gusto that Mr. Moggridge felt he might afford a home away from his shop, and thus he came to take the biggish empty house which presently put on new paint and once more seemed quite proud of being "Zion View."

Till this time, Mr. Moggridge had "attended" elsewhere, but he was not so young as he had been and somewhat stouter, and the stealthy approach of comfortable habits had suggested to him that his old chapel was rather at an unnecessary distance. Then, too, the fact of his house being called after New Zion seemed to impose a sort of obligation towards the sad old chapel. Besides, Mr. Moggridge was not inhumanly above the pleasures of self-importance, and though he did not express it in just those words, or indeed in any words at all, the idea of his being the Mæcenas of New Zion was suddenly born within him.

Now, quick was even the word with Mr. Moggridge, as became a successful man of business, and for him to conceive an idea was to carry it out, as goods were always delivered from Mr. Moggridge's shop, with despatch. Also in some dim far-off way Mr. Moggridge's mind had, all unconsciously, been stirred by vibrations of what we call the New Spirit. The new spirit of any age works its way even into its businesses, and though Mr. Moggridge would n't have so described it, it was the "New Spirit" that had made the success of his provision shop. Speaking of the need of New Zion, Mr. Moggridge called it "new blood." He meant the "New Spirit;" and it was in reply to his advertisement for a new pastor, that the "New Spirit" in the person of Theophilus Londonderry came one Sunday to preach at New Zion.

CHAPTER IV

ENDS QUITE ROMANTICALLY

ELI MOGGRIDGE was a judge of men, and he liked Theophilus Londonderry at a glance. Theophilus Londonderry was also a judge of men, and he liked Eli Moggridge. In fact, two men that needed each other had met.

You couldn't help laughing a little at Mr. Moggridge at first, soon you couldn't help respecting him, — Theophilus Londonderry was almost to know what it was to love him. Indeed, that Mr. Moggridge was just the man he was was a matter of no small importance to the young minister. A chief deacon is nothing less than a fate, and it is in his power to be no little of a tyrant. Had Mr. Moggridge's interest in New Zion been of a different character, he would inevitably have been as great a hindrance as he was to prove a help. Fortunately that interest was recreative rather than severely religious. It was to be for him a sort of Sunday-business to which he was to devote his vast spare energies. He wanted to see it a "going concern," and, hating stagnation in his neighbourhood, he looked about for a specialist whom he could trust to make it move and hum and whizz.

Luckily, in so far as he was an amateur theologian, he was broad, with further mental allowances for expansion. What was wanted at New Zion, he explained to the young minister at supper after the close of an evening service which had more than kept the promise of the morning, was not Dogma, but common-sense every-day religion, a religion to help a man in his business, not a Sunday-coat religion, a cheerful human religion; and it happened that something of this very sort was what Theophilus Londonderry was eagerly prepared to supply.

ZION CHAPEL

The stipend was small, a poor sixty pounds a year, but Mr. Moggridge guaranteed to swell it to a hundred if necessary from his own resources, and he wanted it clearly understood that, short, of course, of the broad general principles of Christian teaching, no restrictions were to be placed either by him or anyone else on the young man's expression of the faith that was in him. "All we want you to do," he said in conclusion, "is to make the place go, give it new blood, new fire; as to how you do it, that is your own business — and I shall no more interfere with you in that than I should expect you to instruct me on the subject of York hams. We must all be specialists nowadays, — specialists," repeated Mr. Moggridge, with a feeling that he too had discovered planets.

So it came to pass that "The Rev. Theophilus Londonderry, Pastor," presently lit up with a sudden vehemence of new goldleaf the faded dusty name board of the chapel, and that, his own home being at too great a distance for his ministrations, he came to lodge with some nice old-fashioned people called Talbot at No. 3, Zion Lane.

I want you to like funny old Mrs. Talbot, and I want you to love her little daughter Jenny; so, to make it the easier, I shall not describe them at too great a length. Old Mr. and Mrs. Talbot were the sole survivors of the less active founders of New Zion, meekly not militantly pious, stubborn as sheep in a dumb obstinacy of ancient faith, but in no sense dialectical, and in every sense harmless.

Mr. Talbot was a working stone-mason, and on rare occasions when front parlour people caught glimpses of him, he was observed to be sitting in the kitchen in some uncomfortable attitude of unoccupation, "like white-haired Saturn, quiet as a stone." It is not recorded that he ever thought on any subject, and it is certain that he seldom spoke. He would flee from a stranger as from a lion, and, when confronted by such from the wilds of the front parlour, he would bob his old head pathetically, and make no attempt at speech beyond a muffled good-evening. It disconcerted him to be expected to speak, and his tongue slumbered in his mouth, — for he was an old weary man, and perhaps very wise.

Old Mrs. Talbot, whose wifehood had long since been submerged in an immeasurable motherhood and the best of cooks, would do the little thinking the house required, take charge of the old man's earnings, pay the rent and the burial club, and scheme little savings against Jenny's marriage — which she kept, not in an old stocking, but in a precious teapot of some old-fashioned ware reputed valuable, and itself carefully wrapped up in a yellow handkerchief of Cashmere. The old lady had a heart of fun in her, and even her notion of romance, and her withered old apple of a face, with its quaint ringleted hair, had once been bonny and red, you might be sure. But she was half blind now, and a good deal deaf, and her sweet old mouth was hard to get at when she kissed you, as she had a motherly way of insisting if she liked you. She, too, was very old, and she, I know, was very wise.

Jenny — well, there is really not much to describe about Jenny, beyond that she was sweetly little, had a winning old-fashioned air about her, was very good, that is, very kind, and was adored by the school-children, whom she taught first for love and then for dress and pocket-money. She was but nineteen, and all unminted woman as yet. No lover had yet come to stamp her features with his masterful superscription. Was she pretty? Heroines ought to be either very pretty or very plain. Well, the beauty that was going to be was as yet only beginning at the eyes. They were already beautiful. No, she wasn't pretty yet, but she wasn't plain.

Jenny's face slept as yet. When the

fairy prince came and kissed it, there was no telling to what beauty it would awake. The fairy prince! That was going to be our friend Theophil, of course. Well, of course, though it's a little early on to admit it. However, I am unequal to the task of concealing from the hawk-eyed reader through a succession of chapters that Jenny and Theophil were to be each other's "fates." Of course, he had n't been there a month before Jenny's face was beginning to wear that superscription of his passionate intelligence, to grow merry from his laughter, and still sweeter by his kisses.

Of course, Theophil and Jenny fell in love. Do you think it was merely to save New Zion and to bring the Renaissance to Coalchester that Theophilus Londonderry was sent to live in Zion Place — or for any other purpose less important than to love Jenny? Yes, we may as well take that for granted as we begin the next chapter.

CHAPTER V

OF THE ARTIST IN MAN AND HIS MATERIALS

THERE is only one way to give life to the dead or the moribund, the way of the Hebrew prophet, — to give it one's own. Theophilus Londonderry instinctively knew this, and he began at once to breathe mightily upon New Zion.

The goldsmith blows merrily all day through his little blowpipe, but it is gold he is working on. The poet breathes upon the dictionary, and lo! it flushes and breaks into flower. But then he is breathing on words. The material of such artists is a joy in itself. They are workers in the precious metals. Theophilus Londonderry had very different material to mould, — an old chapel and some very dull humanity. Humanity is not a precious metal, but if you know how to use it, it is excellent clay, — a clay not without streaks of gold.

What was Theophilus Londonderry's purpose with his material, his will towards the uncreated world over which his young vitalising spirit was moving? To save it? Yes, incidentally; but primarily to express himself by means of it, to set it vibrating to the rhythm of his nature, to set it dancing to a tune of his piping. Already he was being stamped in gold on Jenny's face. The coarser face of the world was to wear his smile too. For the pebble had only been thrown in at New Zion. Who knows to what coasts of fame the imperious ripples of his personality would circle on before they touched the shores of death?

We may be polite as we please to humanity in the mass, and humanity in occasional rarely encountered individuals is — well, divine; and to such we gladly and humbly and rapturously pay divine honours. But in any given thousand human beings, poor or rich, what would be your calculation for the average of such divine, — how many faces would you fall down and worship, how many hands would you care to take, how many hearts would you dare to trust?

Alas, the rather good eyes must go so often with the disastrous chin, the mouth succeed where the nose fails, the expansive impulse be checked by the narrow habit, the little gleam of gold be lost in the clay.

Preponderant charm does not crowd into chapels or anywhere else to be minted, it is busy on some vantage height of its own, impressing its own image; and it is with minds maimed by the cruel machinery of life, natures stunted and starved by adverse and innutritive condition, that the artist in man must be satisfied. With what pathetic little flashes of faculty, what fleeting and illusory glimpses of insight, what waifs and strays of attractiveness, must he work and be happy, and with what a thankfulness that the tenth rate is not twentieth or thirtieth!

Then, too, how often must the intractible material be impressed again and again and again before it begins to wear the first trace of your image. Once a poet has impressed himself with mastery upon words, the impression remains for ever, the words do not disperse in idle crowds when he has done speaking to them, never again to reassemble in a like combination; whereas the greatest oratorical mover of men is doomed, even after his most electrical self-impression, to see his image, as soon as taken, fade away, with a shuffle of escaping feet and a scramble for hats and cloaks. It was a masterpiece; but with the last touch, see, the colours are flying in a hundred directions, and the very canvas itself is off in a thousand threads of hurried disintegration!

But all this, of course, has to do entirely with the poetry of the ministerial life; prosaic even as preaching and praying to the New Zioners may sound, there was yet a drearier prose. For these artistic materials had not only to be preached and prayed to, — they had to be in a measure lived with, listened to, personally studied, and individually considered. Each was an atom to be set in vibration, and each needed to be set or kept going in his own way. All this prose had to be made help in the poetry. How skilful you had to be to rouse the interest you needed and escape the many interests you did not need, to awaken the single gift without bringing upon you all the rest, to suffer the fool wisely, — that is, to the extent of his tiny wisdom, and no more. To encourage say Miss Annie Smith in her district-visiting — what a talent she has for that! — but firmly to forget her at concerts; to welcome Mr. Jones's services at collections, but gently to discourage him at prayer meetings; in short, to meet all at the point where their natures were really and usefully alive, but at no other point of their circumferences.

However, nature had made this as easy as breathing to the Reverend Theophilus, for, apart from his humour and good nature, he was a lover of character for its own sake, and to the student of character there is no such person as a bore. Brother Saunderson was no doubt as wearisome an old man as the world holds, but his manner of neighing to the Lord in prayer was worth it all. And it is rather a pity if the reader imagines that to laugh at his neigh is to forget respect for his venerable faith.

Thus mightily, gently, cunningly, coaxingly, Theophilus Londonderry breathed upon New Zion, and Eli Moggridge was a noble second, according to his word. At every service of every kind, and at all times, he was there, swelling out from a pewful of ruddy daughters, and endlessly beaming round at his fellow-worshippers, as much as to say, "Did n't I say he was the man for New Zion?"

The old channels were beginning to fill with the new spirit, the old disused machinery was once more in motion. In two months' time every possible form of meeting was in a healthy condition of attendance, prayer-meeting, church-meeting, mothers' meeting, Bible class, Dorcas society, Band of Hope, Sunday-school, all briskly in motion; and the ladies, led by Jenny, were all as busy as bees over a bazaar. New Zion had indeed become a veritable merry-go-round of religious and social activities. Yes, it was beginning to move, indeed, it was almost beginning to hum — another few months and it would fairly whizz, as Eli Moggridge had foreseen; and the sound of the humming and the speed of the whizzing would grow louder and louder and faster and faster, till not merely Zion Place and Zion Alley and Zion Passage and Zion Street heard it and were caught up in the infectious dance, but the very High Street itself should hum and whizz.

The High Street! what are High Streets to the soul of Theophilus Londonderry? What is Coalchester itself? — though that shall soon be humming and whizzing too. This is but the whirling centre of the ever-spreading wheel of force that has begun to turn at New Zion. Coalchester will spin soon, and then the disappointed fields around it, then the neighbouring towns would join the reel, and so on and on, faster and faster, madder and madder, till even London itself moves, and the world that changes its axis at the will of any strong spirit will whirl its immeasurable velocities around the vortex pulpit of Theophilus Londonderry.

Yes, the pebble had only been thrown in at New Zion.

CHAPTER VI

OF A WONDERFUL QUALITY IN WOMEN

DARWIN expended many years of his life in the study of disagreeable animals, that he might prove the adaptability of organism to environment. How much pleasanter and briefer had been his task, if he had begun his studies at once with the creature whose long history has been one unbroken succession of inspired and noble adaptations!

Woman's adaptability to man is one of the most mysterious, as it is perhaps the most pathetic, of all the modes of her mysterious being. Like certain protection-seeking animals, she is always the colour of the rock, the husband-rock, in whose shadow she lives. Sometimes, of course, she is her own rock; but in such cases man is never her chameleon to a like degree or indeed in a like manner. Such adaptability is not one of the forms of his greatness, and even when he achieves it, it is not becoming to him.

For woman's adaptability is not the domination of a weaker nature by a stronger, it is in itself a noble and world-necessary form of strength.

Strength is needed as well for the taking as the making of an impression, — something more than mere ductility. Weakness may never bear the stamp of power, — it breaks in the moulding; and it is rather because woman is so strong that she is able to take the Cæsarean stamp of any form of power. Nor cares she by whose hands she is moulded, whose image she wears, be it warrior, poet, or priest, so long as she feels the veritable grasp and impress of power. Some women are already made in the image of the man they are to love before they meet him. Very wonderful, very terrible, then, is the meeting, and it is a meeting that usually comes too late. But oftener God gives a man a little measure of porcelain and a handful of stars, and leaves him to make the woman he needs for himself; and very wonderful too is that making,— though the man will always have been the father before he was the lover.

Why, one may ponder, should a man who is great enough to mould a woman to help him be great, not be great enough to do without her at all? Let lovers of the unfathomable ask at the same time: Why is man, man? and woman, woman? and what are both?

This gentle doll with the sweet breath, which he nips up in his arms and kisses, and gives a tongue that she may talk back to him his own words, endows with brains that she may think his thoughts,— a quaint little helpless lovely parody of his wisdom and power; a toy, yes; a refreshment, yes; a place of peace, yes, — but how much more! Yes, more by all that we don't understand when we say "woman."

Why a great man should need, not a great woman, but a little woman, a very little woman, — how is it to be explained, unless it be that woman, however little, is mysteriously great, just because she is a woman, a little woman? Unknown properties were wrapped up somewhere in that porcelain; to press it with the lips is to feel strange virtue coming into one, — the devil was in those stars.

Great men are only nourished on the elements. Woman is an element, all the elements in one, — earth, air, fire, and water, met together in a rose. She is a spring among the rocks, and she comes up dimpling from the roots of the world. She is just as simple and just as strange. O! little shining spring of woman that is called Jenny, a great man must draw up through you the unfathomed, deep strengths of the old world. He bends above you and drinks, and as he drinks, his face is mirrored in yours.

"Jenny, I don't think I'd read 'Miss

——,' if I were you," would say the great man.

"No, dear?" So Jenny was presently reading Ruskin instead, and wondering how she could ever have read "Miss ——." And deep in her dear heart she was saying, "Of course not; great men's wives never read 'Miss ——.'"

And yet had the great man said, "Read Gaboriau instead," — as a certain very great man does, — Jenny's heart would have said, "Of course, great men's wives always read Gaboriau."

No! great men's wives read "Sesame and Lilies," and "Sartor Resartus," and "Marius the Epicurean," and "Richard Feverel," and "Virginibus Puerisque,"— they even try to read Newman's "Apologia." Such were the books on the sunnier side of Theophilus Londonderry's little library in No. 3 Zion Place. In dark corners behind easy-chairs were the deep-sea pools of theology, — pools which had long since given up all the fish they had in them for their owner, — slabs of antique divinity, such as you would find likewise in the equally cherished library of Londonderry Senior.

Such were the fathers that slumbered on in a well-earned repose, and which, far from desiring new readers, were so old that they were glad to rest undisturbed, — being far too self-important to confuse a considerate regard for their repose with neglect. And many of them were really quite valuable as decoration, because of their fine old coats of gilded leather; and such were ranged in the more penetrable shadows or even in the lamp-light. Theophilus would point to them as to a portrait-gallery of dead ancestors. One might admire the quaint and distinguished cut of their clothes without dreaming of wearing the same, — and indeed old divinity, he used to say, was poor food for young divines.

His divinity indeed was fed on the technical side, it is to be feared, by the more destructive biblical criticism, like most destructive engines, coming all the way from Germany, and at its more vital centres by importations of strong meat from Russia and Scandinavia. Tolstoi and Ibsen were his archprophets.

There was likewise a great Paris moralist called Zola, and a strange old American father called Walt Whitman. And beauty, that can never be far away from strength, found many new and wonderful prophets in that little library, — poets and painters and musicians of whom hardly anyone else in Coalchester had yet heard, and certainly no one above the age of twenty-five.

Surely youth is in nothing more marvellous than in its mysterious power of attracting to itself into the most out-of-the-way places the sustenance and companionship it needs. In the unlikeliest wilderness inspired youth is never without the mysteriously-brought food and the company of angels. Powers of the air will sweep across continents to rescue it from prison, soft gales travel from south to north to sow seeds of beauty in its narrow ways, and little songs will flutter like butterflies for hundreds of miles to cheer its heart.

The Time-Spirit had given its angels charge concerning these young people, and, remote as they were from all the fiery centres of thought and the dreaming schools of art, Zion Place, no less than the Rue de Rivoli, took its thought of the newest and its beauty of the best.

CHAPTER VII

THE LITERARY AND PHILOSOPHICAL
SOCIETY OF COALCHESTER

I HAVE said that Coalchester was a very ignorant old town. I did not mean to imply that there were no M. A.'s there. In fact, there were quite a number. You may be sure that if spiritual and intellectual life had its representatives, as we have seen, spiritual and intellectual death had its representatives, too — by which I don't mean either to imply that the M. A.'s were dead M. A.'s, dead and buried with Latin over them in the old brassed and effigied church, which was so old and large that it was hardly less conceited than a cathedral. Spiritual and intellectual death in Coalchester, as elsewhere, was officially represented by the Literary and Philosophical Society, which still unblushingly went on retaining its adjectives, even in the face of its "Transactions," which seemed mainly composed of treasurer's reports, with an occasional paper on fossils.

Indeed the one spark of life in the pathetic old society was its real interest in the antediluvian and prehistoric. For the life that was dead it had a perfect passion, and it sometimes held conversaziones to gaze at it through microscopes. Occasionally it would waken up to literature with a paper on Akenside. In everything that didn't in the least matter some of these mild old gentlemen were genuinely learned. Not that they hadn't read the great poets, even in the original Greek, Latin, and Italian. Poets in dead and foreign languages were a form of fossils, and English poets — with that divine bloom upon them! — they had a way of fossilising by spectacles, so that they never read them alive. Thus they had never read Shakespeare even in the original.

Once, long ago in Coalchester, a hundred

years ago, there had been a little circle of elegant literati, connoisseurs of literature and art,—men, so far as men of that age might be, genuinely, if timidly and old-maidishly, affectionate towards belles-lettres; men who had got so far as to appreciate the freshness of an Elizabethan song; minor Bishops Percy; and such lavender is the true love of anything that their memories still hung about the walls of the old Lyceum along with their portraits; while so necessary are great names for little towns to boast of, that the compiler of the local gazetteer implied that Coalchester glowed at night with quite a lustre from their names. Besides, they proved very useful in damping young men. And yet you would n't know their names if I were to write them — as I would rather like to do.

The learned Dr. Sibley, he wrote a pleasant little essay on "Taste," you know, with a few additional notes on chiaroscuro; and then there was the learned Dr. Ambrose, who wrote quite a pretty little treatise on Song-writing.

No! Of course you won't know any of them. Yet they were all once, and are still, " The Learned." You'll never hear Theophilus Londonderry spoken of as that, I'm afraid.

As it is the property of fame to grow with time, and the way of a great name to begin with brains and end with lords, a great man's descendants are not unnaturally found persons of much greater consequence than the original great one. In like manner the dignity and importance of the members of the Literary and Philosophical Society had grown, in direct ratio to their distance from the original founders of it; and the learned Doctors Sibley and Ambrose, who really did know something about art and poetry and certainly loved them, can never have been persons of such consequence as one or two of their descendants who are nameless, and who certainly knew nothing about either.

One of the real objects of this sad little Society was passionately to ignore what they contemptuously called local talent. It is true that there was not much to ignore, and, after all, it has now to be recorded to their credit that they did unreservedly give Theophilus Londonderry his chance. By what quaintness of accident he could not imagine, he suddenly found himself invited to lecture before them. The invitation read something like a command, and there seemed to be an implication that if all were satisfactory, he might thus earn the right of acknowledging the patronage of the Literary and Philosophical Society of Coalchester.

Theophilus Londonderry's subject, therefore, was "Walt Whitman,"—a name which conveyed no offence to the Committee, for the simple reason that it conveyed nothing. It was a strange and humorous thing for the young man to think of, that his was to be the first human voice that had spoken that name of the future aloud in Coalchester. As he rose to give his paper, he pronounced its title slowly, with his full carrying voice, and allowed the strange new name to roll away in menacing echoes through the old Lyceum : " W-a-l-t W-h-i-t-m-a-n."

Even yet no one saw the coming doom, heard not the voice that tolled a funeral bell through all Lyceums and other haunted houses of dead learning. The Canon in the chair smiled benignantly, with an expression that I can only compare to buttered rolls. He was just three hundred years old that very day, and the audience (a scanty fifty or so) ran from a hundred and fifty upwards. The only young men present besides the lecturer were two friends of his I have yet to introduce, — Rob Clitheroe, a fiery young poet and pamphleteer of many ambitions, and James Whalley (little James Whalley he was always called) a gentle lover of letters, with perhaps the most delicate taste in the whole little coterie; *and* Mr.

Moggridge, — not entirely comfortable, it having been by some mysterious atmospheric effect conveyed to him that he was a tradesman and a dissenter, in which latter capacity he felt a certain traditional resentment towards his complacent fellow listeners. A quite recent ancestor had refused to pay tithes. That ancestor was in his blood to-night.

Jenny was not there. Ladies were not admitted to the meetings of the Society, there being a sort of implication that masonries of learning, occult sciences of the brain, were practised at their meetings, — matters which never came out in the "Transactions."

The lecture was a straightforward and eloquent account of Whitman's writings and doctrines, with extracts from "The Leaves of Grass;" and from beginning to end you might have heard a pin drop, particularly during one or two of the quotations. When it was ended the buttered-roll expression had faded from the Canon's

ZION CHAPEL 45

face, and his "our young friend" expression was ready for the chairman's remarks. Londonderry's sitting down awakened a few sad echoes that were no doubt handclappings, but seemed like the flapping of the wings of night-birds frightened by a light. But the Lit-and-Phils were not frightened; they were entirely bewildered and rather indignant, that was all. It was characteristic of their incapacity to grasp the humanity of any subject, even when it was dangerous, that the criticism which followed was directed almost entirely against Whitman's metrical vagaries. This was not poetry! Had not their revered founder, the learned Dr. Ambrose . . .

The Canon kindly said, showing his pastoral interest in the local newspaper, that the verses which their young friend Mr. Rob Clitheroe, who was present with them that evening, occasionally contributed to the Coalchester "Argus" were in his opinion better poetry than anything Walt Whitman had written, though he confessed that his acquaintance with Walt Whitman was of the slightest. This disastrous compliment sent the blood to young Clitheroe's cheeks, and he felt surer than ever that he would never be a real poet, — though, as a matter of fact, he had written some quite pretty lines.

It was an occasion that of course only the Lit-and-Phils could take seriously, and the way home to New Zion was a laughter of four beneath the stars, — Mr. Moggridge's deep guffaws coming every now and again, like the bay of some distant watch-dog, at the young minister's brilliant mimicry of the ancient men they had left behind.

Then the gentle voice of little James Whalley took advantage of a silence: "Is n't it high time that we brought the Renaissance to Coalchester?"

"Capital!" cried Londonderry; "come in for a bit of supper, all of you, and let us talk over the plan of campaign."

CHAPTER VIII

THE PLOT AGAINST COALCHESTER

OLD Mrs. Talbot had been prepared for some such invasion, and had an excellent rabbit-pie awaiting them. There was a delightful trait of old Mrs. Talbot's which I would like to record, a curious chronological method of remembering great occasions and startling events by the food of the day. Thus, for example, when with eyes that would still fill with tears, though it was ten years ago, she would tell the story of how her only boy had been brought home dead one night from an accident at his workshop, she would fix the date by saying, " It was about six o'clock at night, and I'd just got a nice little bit of liver and bacon cooking for your father's dinner, when there came a knock at the door . . ." Sometimes it was, "I'd just sent Liz out for a little bit of fish," or it would be Spanish onions maybe, or a lovely little rabbit, that marked the day.

The night when the attack on Coalchester was planned was marked, as I have said, by rabbit-pie. Mrs. Talbot would hardly have understood the significance of that rabbit-pie, though in the course of her occasional bobbings in and out of the room, to see that the young men were doing justice to her food, — she had a curious notion that young men never ate enough, — she would hear snatches of what she called "deep talk," or shake her old head at her coming son-in-law, whom she already adored and mothered, with a "Law! what a boy it is!" She was n't quite sure sometimes as to the soundness of his "doctrine," but wisely decided that her business was rather with his stomach than his brains, — which no doubt God Almighty would look after for himself.

Wit at the expense of Coalchester can

ZION CHAPEL 49

only be of interest to Coalchester wits and their butts, so I shall not record the bright and animated talk which helped to digest Mrs. Talbot's rabbit-pie, but confine myself to a practical outcome of it.

What interests me specially about these young men was their rare practicality. They were no mere dreamers, helpless visionaries, with ideas they had no notion how to embody. Dreamers, of course, they were,—otherwise there had been no point in their being practical,—but they were dreamers who understood something of how dreams are best got on to the market of realities.

Characteristically, it was the poet of the party from whom the most practical suggestion came. In itself, of course, there was no great originality in the idea of a weekly paper to be called "The Dawn," devoted to the dissemination of the new light on every possible subject,—politics and municipal misgovernment; the new social ideals; the newest and most delicate forms of art, music, and literature. It was in the suggested method of publication and circulation that the originality lay. The paper was to be given away and made to pay its expenses by tradesmen's advertisements, a guarantee of a certain minimum distribution being given. This method had, of course, been tried before for purposes of mere publicity, but never, I think, for the dissemination of truth and beauty. The truth about life was to be paid for by lies about bacon and butter,—or, let us say, business exaggerations rendered innocuous by custom, and therefore as harmless as truth.

Obviously Mr. Moggridge, who not unnaturally had felt a sense of moving about in worlds not realised during much of the deep talk, was here an authority of importance, and the idea at once appealed to him. He would promise a permanent advertisement, and he even promised illustrations, in the form of blocks already engraved and occasionally used by the

"Argus," of the flourishing shops at 33, 34, 35 High Street, and 58, 59 Zion Street. He had also some blocks of gigantic hams most hammily pictured, which might also be of use, and he would also be able to bring in a number of his fellow tradesmen. Invaluable Mr. Moggridge! What were truth without you!

The poet, on his part, guaranteed to supply all the poetry that might be required, and indeed agreed to do special rhyming advertisements, at, say, half a guinea apiece. He would also assist Londonderry in the political and municipal departments, not only in the higher flights, but lend a hand even in castigations of local jobs, abuses, and absurdities.

Gentle James Whalley would write roundabout essays, for which he had a charming gift, and generally take in charge the æsthetic interests of the paper, though, as all were lovers of art and literature, those subjects would be handled now by one and now by another. Even Jenny was to have her place on the staff, and write dress articles, which would not only tend to improve the aspect of Coalchester streets, but attract millinery advertisements. She already announced the title of her first article, which was very grand: "Dress as a form of self-expression."

It was two in the morning before the proceedings terminated, and even then good old Mrs. Talbot was still up to press steaming bumpers of very hot whisky and water upon the wayfarers; "to keep the cold out," she explained — though I need hardly say that the project had not waited till that hour to be suitably recommended to the god of all enterprises.

CHAPTER IX

"THE DAWN."

NEXT to the delight of holding new and unpopular opinions is the delight of having a medium for their unedited expression, though this is a delight given to few reformers. "The Dawn," however, was to be such a medium; and when the first number appeared, as it did nearly a month from the meeting recorded in the last chapter, four people, nay, five — for we must n't forget Mr. Moggridge — were supremely happy. With the exception of the poet, who, as we have seen, occasionally irradiated the poet's corner of the "Argus," and Mr. Moggridge, it was a first appearance in print for three out of the five contributors; and though each talked most of the articles by the others, they were secretly longing to get away with the little paper to some corner where they could gloat over their own special contribution.

Not that they had any ridiculous ideas of the literary importance of the articles in question, but because it seemed so strange to see the warm words of their mouths thus condensed into cold print, so strange to think that people all over Coalchester were reading them. Little Jenny in particular felt quite a cold but pleasant shiver of notoriety as she thought of it, while to her lover the delighted perusal and reperusal of a large-type leading article, headed " In Darkest Coalchester! " brought a new sense of power.

The poet, as was only to be expected, had his little grievance with the printer, who, in spite of all his remonstrances and corrections in proof, — the printer was a little wrong-headed Scotchman, — had insisted at the last moment in heading his Tyrtean " Proem," a fine aerial trumpet-blast somewhat Shelleyan in style, with the

ZION CHAPEL

word that was evidently intended, namely, "Poem." However, he was somewhat consoled by reading his caustic column of notes headed "The World outside Coalchester," the very heading of which was a revelation. Then, too, he very much enjoyed his article on "Bad Lighting in Coalchester," with its evident allegoric insinuation that Coalchester needed lighting in more ways than one, and that "The Dawn" was prepared to undertake, free of charge, the top-lighting of which it was most in need.

James Whalley contributed a review of "Mr. Swinburne's new Poems," through which article Mr. Moggridge's illustrated hams plainly showed from the other side.

New truth is too often printed in very worn-out type, but the promoters of "The Dawn" had wisely remembered how hard truth is to read, and had given it good clear type, and generally made it a very comely and attractive little paper. It bore a motto that sounded almost like a threat,

"We come to stay," — a boast which it manfully kept for several years. As I lift my eyes from this paper, they rest on no less than ten great half-yearly volumes, which flash "The Dawn" — "The Dawn" — along a darksome folio shelf, as they have flashed it week after week across darkest Coalchester; and "The Dawn" ceased, at length, not from lack of power and encouragement to continue, but because the world had grown sadder by then, and it had lost the will to go on living.

In spite of this hardy existence, I suppose "The Dawn" will win no record of itself in the histories of the press, though merely as spirited journalism it deserves to do so; while in the history of the human spirit at Coalchester it demands a grateful celebration such as it will, again, most surely not receive from the literary and philosophical historian of the town. At all events, honoured or forgotten as it may be, should you ever come across its strange young pages, I know you will agree with me that it was a wonderful little paper. It was not, you may suspect, conservative, being, as it was, very alive and very young. In fact, its radiant radicalism brings tears to one's eyes to-day, when so many of the noble ideals it championed, to the length and strength of its little angry arm, are lying smashed beneath the iron blows of the capitalism that has outlived even the noble eloquence of Theophilus Londonderry.

Like all young people, it was all for the young, the new; and I think you will be astonished, if you do ever turn over its pages, at the remarkable instinct for the crescent life possessed by these young men; and, were it worth while, I could easily prove that several of the more exquisite continental writers, now the fashion this many a year, first found a humble welcome in that quaint little organ of New Zion.

Yes! it was a triumph for New Zion too. This modest and hitherto obscure corner of the town suddenly found itself, comparatively, in a blaze of publicity, for a column headed "Work at New Zion," evidently meant to be weekly, left no doubt from what quarter of the town the dawn was to be looked for. This was perhaps the most delightful thing about the paper,—its calm assumption that the real aristocracy of the town was to be found in that little back street, and that, if Coalchester was to have any spiritual or intellectual life, it must seek it there. In Zion Street, and nowhere else in Coalchester, were the angels descending into the waters. And the best part of the joke was that the assumption was literally true.

CHAPTER X

HOW THEY BROUGHT THE GOOD NEWS OF A MORRIS WALL-PAPER TO COALCHESTER

COALCHESTER was too much taken by surprise by "The Dawn" to pretend to ignore it, and its first recognition was appropriately made in a ludicrously abusive article in "The Argus,"— "the one-eyed Argus," as it was mockingly nicknamed in the next week's issue of the new paper. The joke was one that was lost on Coalchester, which had never dreamed of expecting a hundred eyes in its "Argus," which to it was but the usual name for a sleeping newspaper. It was, however, to do them justice, seen and chuckled over by one or two members of the Literary and Philosophical Society. "The young beggars know their — classical dictionary, at all events," said one of them maliciously, which was quite bright for a Lit-and-Phil.

One tangible result of the little paper was the almost immediate doubling of the attendance at New Zion. Curiosity had been aroused in this militant young minister with the strange ideas, and Theophilus Londonderry wished for nothing better than to gratify it. In the oxygen of success even the dullest metals will scintillate, and it needed but such small beginnings of his future to make Theophilus as nearly irresistible as natural gifts and success together can make a man.

Some people go to chapel to worship, a few to learn, but most, odd as it may sound, to be entertained. A vivid and magnetic preacher is as near as many will allow themselves to approach the theatre. Theophilus was a born actor — of himself; a part so few can or dare play. He gave you good stimulating truth; but it was not so much in the newness of the ideas which

ZION CHAPEL

he passed on from his books to his hearers, as in the newness of himself, that of course the charm lay. A few people, not many or important, disliked him; but all had to listen, and a good many came to New Zion again. Above all, the women heard him gladly; and to this sure sign of a future Theophilus was far from blind. "He has women at his back, he cannot fail," was a phrase he sometimes recalled out of his favourite *Brand*. Yes, and had he not one little angel-woman at his side?

It had been the spring of 1886 when he came to New Zion. It was now the autumn, and early in September announcements had been made of a series of autumnal lectures to be given by the Rev. Theophilus Londonderry; Rob Clitheroe, Esquire; James Whalley, Esquire; and other distinguished lecturers, at New Zion.

In the list were papers on "The Duty of Novel Reading," "Henrik Ibsen," "A Morris Wall-Paper," "The Nude in Art," and "The Darwinian Theory," by Mr. Londonderry himself; "Coalchester, its Past and its Future," by Mr. Rob Clitheroe; together with "Ireland's Sacred Right to Home Rule," by the same lecturer; "Wagner and the New Music," by Mr. James Whalley, with a paper on "Some Really New Books," by the same; and a paper on "Good Taste in Dress," by Miss Jenny Talbot — the virago!

The batteries were to be turned on poor Coalchester with a vengeance. For some time past there had been uneasy suspicions in the town that strange and somewhat ungodly forms of new learning and beauty were being stored as in an arsenal in that little house at 3 Zion Place. A large cast of the Venus of Milo, it was known, had come from Covent Garden, London, *via* a poor little dealer in artistic materials in the town, who on one occasion had shown a bewildering picture to one of his customers with the remark, "What do you make of this, Mr. Littlejohn?"

Mr. Littlejohn could make nothing of it, nor indeed could the artists' colourman, who had been used to pictures all his life.

No wonder, for it was the first Rossetti that had ever been seen in Coalchester.

And it was the same at the little paperhanger's shop where Theophilus had ordered some pieces of Morris wall-paper for his room.

"Law! what a taste, to be sure!" had exclaimed the paperhanger's wife as they opened the parcel. "How any one dare live with such patterns is beyond me." The paperhanger's wife verbed better than she knew. Few are those indeed who dare live with beauty.

When the paper was hung in Theophil's room, so great was the sensation in the household that even old Mr. Talbot ventured to look in at it, keeping very close to his wife. It was so the old man had stood open-mouthed before the first steam-engine, and here again was the Devil plainly at work.

"Lord a-mercy, Jane," he said to his wife, "what is the world coming to?"

The world was indeed changing beneath the old man's feet, and the heavens opening as never before in his time — with, he might be right, some assistance from beneath; and — it was undoubtedly safer in the kitchen.

Mrs. Talbot in these matters lived and loved by faith in her boy, as she called him. But even she had her doubts, which she expressed in a way that showed, funny old woman as she was, that she was not without a sort of blind insight.

"I suppose it's all right, boy," she said, "and it sounds silly to say about a lot of harmless lines and flowers, but it seems to your old mother that there's something wrong about that paper, — something almost wicked in it. It reminds me of that nasty music you and Jenny are so fond of playing."

Here Theophil enveloped her in a huge hug, and laughingly mocked her with playful caresses, smiling to himself all the same. For the music she had referred to was Dvorak.

CHAPTER XI

A LITTLE ABOUT JENNY

MEANWHILE, as New Zion moved and hummed and whizzed, and as " The Dawn " went on dawning week by week, — you could n't expect the dawn oftener than once a week in Coalchester, — the love of Jenny and Theophil grew more and more perfect.

There was a long while to wait yet before Jenny was to bear what seemed to her the finest of all names, for old Mrs. Talbot, easily manageable as a rule, had a way of quietly putting her foot down on occasion that would have surprised you. Jenny was only just passed nineteen, and was no fit wife for any man yet, least of all for a great sprawling fellow like that. Let her get a little more flesh on her bones, something more than all spirit and nerves, let her get well turned twenty, and it might be thought of, but not now.

No! it's no use coming with your nonsense, you silly big fellow! You know when the soft old mother says a thing, she means it.

So it proved. Old Mrs. Talbot on this point remained a homely form of adamant. However, the lovers were not badly off. Living in the same house, they saw almost as much of each other as if they had been married, and from the evenings she spent there, Jenny had come to regard Theophil's room and his books as hers too.

She had developed wonderfully in these months, had Jenny. She was a real little great man's wife now; and as Theophil looked at her, with her lit eager face, her whole soul so alive to help him in however humble a way, her whole life his, his, his, — such love seemed almost tragic in its very beauty and joy. It was so irremediably — love. At times he almost trembled before it. He would almost chide her with its divine completeness.

What if he were to be taken from her? Oughtn't she to keep just a little of herself for foothold? We ought all to belong to ourselves as well as to another. It was such a risk. Suppose he were to die, Jenny!

No doubt it was very wise, but Jenny was wiser. She could never belong to herself again. She was his, and his only, for ever; and if he died — if he were to be taken away . . .

But he could never be taken from her any other way? No one else, nothing but death, could take him . . .

"No, nothing but death — and perhaps not even death."

"You are sure, darling? O, you are quite, quite sure?"

"Sure from my soul, little child. Look in it and see."

A lover's eyes are his soul.

Yes, Theophil loved Jenny, loved her

even more with her own dependence on love than he knew of. He was, the reader need scarcely be told, an almost wildly ambitious man, and a few months ago he would have said that there was nothing which was more to him than the expression of the power that was in him. But there was something that was even more to him now, and if it could be imagined that he might some day be asked to choose between his ambition and Jenny, he could honestly have answered from his soul, " Give me Jenny."

Whoever thinks this an easily natural answer to make, may know something about love, but evidently knows little about ambition. Still, life seldom sets us such silly examination questions as that, and need one say that that question was never put to Jenny's lover? He was far too proud of the woman he had made of that little measure of porcelain and that handful of stars.

CHAPTER XII

HOW THE RENAISSANCE CAME IN PERSON TO NEW ZION

THE winter months had gone by; all but one of those incendiary lectures had been given, not without storm and tempest; "The Dawn" still came up each week with anger and singing, and the first year of Londonderry's ministry at New Zion neared its close. The lecture season was presently to end, on the last Friday in March, with a concert which was to include a series of recitations by a lady-reciter from London. Londonderry had written to a lecture agency for the name of a likely reciter, man or woman, and they had sent him the name of Isabel Strange.

On the occasion of the last lecture, Mr. Moggridge had not been satisfied with the colour of the platform. It wanted repainting, and I think it very likely that it was a strain of that boyishness which I hope survives in us all, and one of whose quaint fancies is an envy of house-painters, so happy all day with paint-pot and brush and great smooth boards to dab and smooth, that decided him to do the job himself. Mr. Moggridge had this great element of refinement, that he thought nothing honest beneath him.

It was the Friday of the entertainment, about one o'clock, and though Mr. Moggridge had practically finished the work the day before, he had slipped in during his lunch-hour to give it a final touch or two. He had brought his lunch in the form of a pork-pie, and while with one hand he plunged the pie occasionally among his red whiskers, with the other he would lean forward and touch up a knot or a nail-hole that needed a little more paint. And he was proud as a boy of the simple bit of slap-dashing, and entirely absorbed in it and the pork-pie.

Presently he became aware that he was not alone. Someone had entered the schoolroom at the far end. He turned round, with the paint-brush in one hand and the pork-pie in the other, and became abashed, for a beautiful lady had entered the room and was evidently about to make an enquiry. The surreptitiousness that seems to inhere in pork-pies prompted Mr. Moggridge to slip the pie into his trousers' pocket — for his coat was off, and a white apron had taken its place.

"Just doing a little bit of amateur painting," he explained rather awkwardly, advancing to the lady.

"So I see," said the lady, with a pleasant smile. "This, I believe, is Zion Chapel — and I suppose this is the room where I am to recite. My name is Isabel Strange, and I have come a little earlier, I daresay, than you expected; but I always like to see the room I'm to recite in — just to try my voice in and run over my pieces."

ZION CHAPEL

"Certainly, of course," said Mr. Moggridge; "but you have come all the way from London and so early. You will have some refreshment first, and if you'll honour Mrs. Moggridge and me — I may as well explain that I am the chief deacon," said Mr. Moggridge, dexterously slipping off his painter's apron and getting into his coat. So, with a wistful glance at his work of art, Mr. Moggridge carried off the beautiful London lady to Zion View.

But was Isabel Strange beautiful? It was a new sort of beauty if she was — or perhaps a very old sort. Yet beautiful was the first word that had sprung into Mr. Moggridge's mind as she had surprised him in the schoolroom. Perhaps wonderful was the exacter word, wonderful in a way that included beauty, — wonderful, and with a strange air about her that suggested exceptional refinement, exquisite sensitiveness to refined things.

"Beautiful, O dear no!" said Mrs. Moggridge, to whom feminine beauty did not appeal, as the young lady freshened herself up after her travel in Mrs. Moggridge's best bedroom. "Why! she has n't a regular feature in her face!"

Mrs. Moggridge herself had neat little pretty features set in fat.

"Look at that long upper lip and her nose!"

Mrs. Moggridge omitted mention of eyes singularly powerful and very true and sweet, as also of a long lithe mouth that reminded you of a beautiful serpent, a serpent which the true eyes plainly said would do you no harm.

Presently, however, Mrs. Moggridge had to admit that she was very attractive. She knew she meant fascinating, but she would n't admit that to Mr. Moggridge, who had dropped the subject; though a mind which again had asserted its dim preference for new fashions was perhaps groping after expression of some such perplexity as this: why, if a face has the same effect upon you as beauty, may it not be described as beautiful? If Mr. Moggridge really got so far even as cloudily to ponder that, it is evident that he was not far from the kingdom of beauty.

It is, of course, true enough that some faces are spoilt by flaws such as every Mrs. Moggridge can point out, — faces that begin in one style and end in another, half Greek perhaps and half Gothic; yet even such faces, if their individuality is strong enough, have their own rococo charm. For all but supremely great faces, of which perhaps the world has not seen half-a-dozen, absolute regularity, so-called correctness, of features is a calamity, and regular beauty on the ordinary human levels is only another form of mediocrity.

Wonderful English girls! face after face indistinguishable from each other as rose after rose. How sweet you are! how fragrant! what a bloom! It is a wonderful rose-girl-farm from which you come. How pretty you look laced up one after another on your standards, and how skilfully you are guarded against any form of variation! Perhaps no women potteries in the world produce so exquisite a surface, delicate as a lily and strong as marble. Indeed you are wonderful porcelain, you fair English girls, wonderful porcelain; but where are the stars?

Mrs. Moggridge had also remarked that Miss Strange was "very easy in her manners." This was not always the case with ladies in Coalchester, and Mrs. Moggridge did not mean the remark as an unreserved compliment. She liked a certain stiffness in strangers. It was not, however, in Isabel Strange's nature to oblige her in that particular. Her way of pouring her grace into Mrs. Moggridge's great arm-chair suggested at once that she had lived there for ever so long, and to him particularly she chatted as with an old acquaintance. You could not make a stranger of her. She ate some cold fowl which presently appeared, entirely without embarrassment, though two Miss Moggridges sat like dummies and watched her.

"That's an interesting face!" she said presently, pointing to a conspicuous portrait of a young man on the mantelpiece.

"That's Mr. Londonderry," said Mr. Moggridge.

"O! *that*'s Mr. Londonderry, is it?" she said. "H'm, . . . I hadn't expected him to be so young."

"Yes! He's a wonderful young man for his position," said Mr. Moggridge, started on what was now his favourite topic. "He'll be a great man some day, will Mr. Londonderry."

Isabel looked up at Mr. Moggridge with added interest. Such a genuine interest in great men as his voice betokened was a surprise in him.

Then Mr. Moggridge proceeded to narrate the history of New Zion, told of its former desolation, his lucky advertisement, and its present prosperity.

"Yes, it was a dead-and-alive place was

New Zion when we moved in here, was n't it, missus?" turning to his wife; "but now, since Mr. Londonderry came, there is always something moving. Yes, there's always something going on at New Zion," he repeated, rubbing his hands gleefully. Mr. Moggridge did so love anything that was alive.

Mr. Moggridge also told the story of "The Dawn," and generally, as he would have said, posted her up in the position of things at New Zion. At the end she found herself generally looking forward to meeting this young minister and his friends, who were evidently a little nest of surprise-people in what had indeed seemed a most unpromising corner of the world, — perhaps the most unpromising corner that her nomadic wandering minstrel existence had brought her to.

Isabel Strange, according to old-fashioned reckoning, was not a very young woman. That is, she was already twenty-eight, though, having to fight a silly world with its own silly weapons, she called herself twenty-five, which it was still quite safe for her to do; and though the nerve-intensity of her face was the worst thing in the world for wrinkles, they would when they came be very interesting wrinkles, and her eyes and mouth would keep the world from looking at the rest of her features for a long time to come. A face so full of the mystery of light could only be eclipsed by one darkness, and even in that those magnetic eyes would shine through the cold closed lids.

Surprises were welcome to her, for she got few. Her life was rather a dreary one, as the life of an elocution teacher may well be. At one time she had dreamed of the stage, but her voice was not quite big enough for that, some managers had said, and indeed her mettle was perhaps a little too fine for the stage. The positive and enduring joys of her life were that she lived in London — for which she had the kind of passion that some people have for the Earth-Mother — and loved beauty as some women love religion. She had been loved many times, but never quite as she needed, as she demanded, to be loved. Vivid, passionate, and exquisite, she was what we call "modern" to the tips of her beautiful fingers; that is, she united the newest opinions on all things with many ancient charms. At the same time she was a good woman, though very wonderful and highly dangerous.

Presently Mr. Moggridge, who from where he sat commanded a view of the street, exclaimed, "Why, here is Mr. Londonderry himself!" rising as he spoke and passing into the hall, where he was met by a curiously rich and mellow voice, which Isabel Strange thus heard for the first time; and then the glorified original of the photograph entered the room.

As her eyes and hands met his, her soul gave a little half-humorous "Oh!" of surprise; for photography, which seems to have been invented to flatter the mediocre and belittle the exceptional, had indeed given Londonderry an "interesting face," as we have heard, but missed all the rest —" all the rest " of a large, mobile, talking face, not exactly handsome perhaps, but decidedly good-looking and full of various commands and appeals, thought on the brow and laughter in the eyes, humour and eloquence all along the large and somewhat loose mouth, with plenty of go in the powerful but not anxiously determined chin. These were the moral qualities of the face, which Isabel Strange did not miss; but it was the fascination of its general vitality that struck her most, as an important introduction was made, to the usual fantastic accompaniment of small talk.

Let us not prolong the small-talk of the situation further, but introduce Miss Strange as speedily as possible to Jenny also and to the little study in 3 Zion Place.

Here her eager examination of the shelves was one succession of cries of sympathetic delight. "Why, you have got all the books I ever want to read again!" she exclaimed. "What wonderful people you are! How have you done it — in Zion Place?"

"I suppose the books must have been blown here," answered Theophil, gaily, "on the same fair wind that blew Miss Isabel Strange."

"Yes," said little Jenny, affectionately pressing her shoulder as the three leaned forward looking at the shelves, "for if we seem wonderful people to you, what must you seem to us — here, as you may well say, in Zion Place?"

"What *does* she remind you of?" said Jenny presently, with candid admiration. "I know! Why, of course, she just *is* the very woman. Wait — I'll go and fetch it;" and Theophil and Isabel were thus left for a moment or two alone, — a fact of no importance beyond this, that it was the first moment in their lives that they had ever been together alone.

Jenny returned presently with a small copy of Botticelli's "Primavera," which hung in her bedroom; and it was undoubtedly true that the figure of Flora might well have passed for a portrait of Isabel. The nose was a little longer, that was all; but the rest of the face — particularly the eyes and mouth — was all but exact, and the general correspondence between the two faces in subtlety, strangeness, and, so to say, determined refinement, was complete.

"It is strange that I should have loved that face so," said Jenny.

"It is very sweet of you, — Jenny, I had almost said, — but you are too kind to me, and a little selfish too — you give me no time to admire you. I wonder if Mr. Londonderry is modern enough to allow ladies to smoke in his study."

And thus it comes out that Jenny often smoked there!

The smoking-sister is now almost as common as a taste for Botticelli, and perhaps equally insincere; but in 1886 there still remained that sense of contrast in both which we have declared the essence of romance. At present those curious people who resent the popular acceptance of an ideal of beauty which they have done their best to popularise are beginning to affect that a taste for Botticelli is a mark of the *bourgeoisie*. So does the whirligig of time bring in the paradoxer.

A new kind of woman, while she is always the despairing hope of men, is seldom acceptable to women; yet when the evening came and Isabel stood up to recite in New Zion schoolroom, women as well as men were instantaneously attracted. She stood very simply, with one hand lightly touching the table at which Londonderry sat as chairman, and the other at her side; and before she began her first recitation she glanced quietly over the audience, as though her eyes were thus preparing the proper magnetic atmosphere for her voice.

ZION CHAPEL

She began with some simple Longfellow poem, that New Zion might feel at home; then she recited a fairy poem called "The Forsaken Merman," which, of course, was only a fairy tale, and yet somehow was so full of human pathos that it was more real than if it had been really "real," that is, prosaic.

For impressing the imagination of her audience she relied mainly on her own imagination and her voice; striking no attitudes, and allowing herself nothing of that facial distortion which is the resort of the unimaginative, and destroys not creates illusion. Of course, her face changed, but the change was one of which she was probably unconscious, and which she couldn't have reproduced to her mirror; it was not a play of features, but a play of lights and shadows and nerves, a flow or an ebb of radiance in the eyes, a subtle sensitiveness of the lips and nerves; and her effect was mainly produced by her voice, over which she wielded indescribable powers of modulation. It was a voice so sympathetic, so intimate, that it almost seemed too intimate, too appealingly sympathetic. It was so a woman might recite to a man she loved, but you almost felt as though the voice were too personal a revelation for an audience,—felt an impulse, so to say, to throw a veil over it, though you were glad from your soul that no one threw it.

And the voice was a wonderful actor too. It could act the scenery as well. You saw it all, you heard it all, you felt it all, in the voice:—the great winds blowing shorewards, the wild white horses in the spray,

> "The white-walled town,
> And the little gray church on the windy shore;"

and when she said, "Down, down, down!" you were indeed in the very depths of the sea—and were all sitting, Mr. Moggridge with the rest, amid coral caves and seaweed, and in a curious green and shimmering light.

ZION CHAPEL

But what a world of heart-break there was in her " Come, dear children, come away!" You felt you simply could n't bear her to say it again. Next time you 'd have to cry, and cry you did, and you were n't ashamed, for suddenly when you came out of the trance of the voice you found that every one else was crying too, and Mr. Londonderry had quite forgotten that he was a chairman, and had to be nudged to announce the next piece.

This was a very strange poem, and made you feel like a stained-glass window; it was full of incense, but it was full of something else too. It began

" The blessed damozel leaned out
From the gold bar of heaven " . . .

and there was something in the voice that suggested such a height up above the world that you drew your breath lest she should fall over. And there was a lover crying in the poem, you could hear him crying far away down on the earth, and there were some lines which went:

> "We two will lie i' the shadow of
> That mystic living tree
> Within whose secret growth the Dove
> Is sometimes felt to be" . . .

that made you feel what a strange holy thing love was, after all; and then there was a curious verse with nothing but women's names in it, yet somehow it seemed the loveliest of all; and when again you came out of the voice, you were not crying but feeling wonderfully blest somehow and rather frightened. Jenny sent a wonderful look to Theophil — it was so they should bathe together in God's sight — and Theophil sent back as wonderful a look as a chairman dare venture on. Otherwise, of course, it would have been as wonderful as Jenny's.

Thus did Isabel Strange recite at New Zion; and perhaps one can best judge of the impression she made, from the fact that the little boys at the back, who during the last lecture on "Henrik Ibsen" had discovered a most exciting new way of making continued existence possible, quite forgot it and would have to keep it for Sunday afternoon Sunday-school.

Everyone went home in a dream, and little Jenny shone like a light with the excitement and wonder of it all.

"How wonderful you are! Does n't it seem strange to be so wonderful?" said Jenny afterwards, as the two girls took off their outdoor things in Jenny's room.

"Dear child!" said Isabel, kissing Jenny on her brow, "it is you that are wonderful."

There is no joy in the world better worth seeing, better worth living, than the joy of young people with the same dreams, the same thoughts, and — so important — the same words for them, blown together by some unexpected conjunction of the four winds, met by some blissful dispensation of the planets of youth.

There have been periods in history especially favourable for the ecstasy of such meetings, early mornings of the human spirit, when lovely new truth and lovely new beauty were dawning wild and dewy in the strange east, and while the deep breathing of the older generations still asleep made a more wonderful loneliness of dawn, for the hushed and happy bands of young people holding each other's hands and watching in the magic twilight.

To have been young in Italy in the time of Dante, in England in the time of Shakespeare, and to have met in such a mighty morning — with danger too to keep us grateful. Ah, we have missed those dawns; and yet I doubt if the whole recovered beauty of Greece and Rome, or the thrilling new fashions in romance and poetry wafted across the seas from Italy to help make Shakespeare, ever gave young people a keener thrill of newness and mystery than the books and pictures so eagerly discussed by the little group that gathered over supper that night in 3 Zion Place.

To have read "The House of Life!"—
to have seen the "Venus Verticordia"!
Ah! that was life! And Isabel had
actually been to Mr. G. F. Watts's studio — walked about there a whole afternoon. The young New Zioners looked
at her.

"O Theophil, we *must* go to London,"
cried Jenny. She meant when they were
married.

Theophil pressed her hand tenderly, as
she impulsively sought his for sympathy,
and his eyes left Isabel's face a moment to
smile a true "yes" into Jenny's.

Of course no one had eyes for anyone
but Isabel that night. Was she not, as the
announcements had said, "of London," an
ambassadress of beauty from the capital of
the great queen? There was really little
she could tell these clever young people,
who amazed and attracted her by their
reality, — the unrealities of "intensity"
and "modernity" and the rest had, of
course, already begun in London, — but she

represented to them the sparkle of the new beauty and truth they loved. She knew little intimate anecdotes of the poets and painters they loved, piquant gossip and brilliant *mots;* and then she was one of those women who are like incense in a room, enriching by her very presence, exhaling mystery and distinction, like a pomander of strange spices.

You might love her for a long time or a little, but love her you were obliged to while you were with her, whoever else you loved too. There was no other word for it. Even little James Whalley had conscience-pangs as he looked at Isabel, for he had been engaged for five years; but the poet's heart, that is, all the combustible portion of it, was already burnt to a cinder. Poets' hearts, however, are used to burning. The inflammable air of sighs about them is ever in a perpetual state of ignition; so it has come, no doubt, from long custom, that nature has made them at their centre as fireproof as the phœnix.

Otherwise, indeed, the poetic life would be impossible to live; poets could not go on maintaining the deadly fire of love, to which it is one of the conditions of their precarious art that they must daily expose themselves. Sometimes, indeed, as we know, even these firemen of the emotions dare the burning house once too often, and we hear their death-song amid the flames.

Theophil?

Well, we can talk of Theophil again. Meanwhile Jenny was as much in love with her herself, and he held Jenny's hand and loved her, O yes, so dearly — and was quite safe. Fear not, little Jenny; it was only death, you remember, that was to separate Jenny and Theophil.

Mrs. Talbot — if she won't bore you — had made an interesting remark. She had not escaped Isabel's charm, but there was "something," something a little alarming about her, — a little like that wicked wallpaper.

Jenny divulged this criticism over supper when her mother was out of ear-shot.

"How very clever of her!" exclaimed Isabel.

"She said the same of Dvorak's music," said Jenny.

"Good again," said Isabel. "How clever of her! Don't you feel how right she is? We are all like that wall-paper, and everything we care about is like it. The New Spirit — that is, the devil — is in that wall-paper. A psychometrist could detect Wagner and Keats, and Schopenhauer, and Rossetti and Swinburne, and all the rest of them in that wall-paper, just as surely as he could have detected Tupper and Eliza Cook in the wall-papers of 1851. Am I not right?"

"If we could only paper New Zion like this!" exclaimed Theophil, a curious new feeling of joy and pain shooting through him to hear a woman thus expressing herself as an independent brain.

"Yes! New Zion! I'd quite forgotten

all about New Zion. It seems impossible to think of you together."

"And a little absurd, I suppose," said Theophil.

"It is uncouth material, I admit," he continued, "and yet somehow it amuses us to mould it all the more; and then you must n't forget that we had been given no other — but I don't suppose you can understand?" (Theophil often used "we" in this imperatorial sense, meaning himself, as of course he had every right to mean.)

"O yes, but I can," Isabel hastened to correct. "I understand power."

"Beauty always does," was the young minister's reply.

"Besides," he presently resumed, "we are glad to have been Nonconformists — once. A Puritan training is a good thing — to look back upon. You are all the more thorough in your pleasures, the truer humanist, for something of it still lurking in your blood."

"Yes, of course you're right. I don't

like the word 'pagan'; but for want of a better, we might say that the best pagans have come of Puritan stock. Besides, it is half the romance of life to have something to escape from, isn't it?"

"And someone to escape with the other half," responded Theophil, nimble as a real town wit.

O it was a wonderful night. Let us build five tabernacles!

"Good-night, dear Jenny."

"Good-night, dear wonderful Isabel."

So at last the two girls bade each other good-night at the door of Jenny's bedroom, where Isabel was to sleep.

Masterful youth! So wild to take, so eager to surrender, the Christian name. Strange, what passion sometimes can be put into a *Christian* name!

When the door was shut on Isabel, she made no haste to undress. Indeed, she sat down on the side of the bed as though she had been waiting to sit down for ever so long, sat very still as in a dream, and an hour went by and she was still sitting and gazing in front of her.

And downstairs in the study, where the lamps were still burning, Theophil was sitting by the fire in just the same curiously wrought and withdrawn way, with just the same eyes.

Isabel's room was over his. Presently she heard him moving about; then she heard him coming upstairs. For a moment the air seemed to grow warm, as she heard him softly pass her room; then she heard him close his door.

She shook her reverie from her, as though it had been a black veil full of stars, and began to undress. Presently her eyes fell on a little pile of handkerchiefs, with needle and cotton, and little letters printed on dainty tapes, beside it. Jenny had forgotten to put away her sewing.

Isabel took up one of the handkerchiefs, to which the needle and thread were still attached, and read "Jenny Lond . . ." (Don't you know that's bad luck, Jenny?)

"So soon as that! Is it so soon as that?" she sighed.

Happy Jenny!

CHAPTER XIII

IN WHICH JENNY KISSES MR. MOGGRIDGE

ISABEL was leaving very early next morning for London, so good-byes must be brief. Jenny and Theophil saw her off at the station, but before leaving Zion Place there had been a moment in which for the second time in their lives she and Theophil had been alone.

They had stood together in the little study and taken each other's hands, without a word, and they had looked into each other's faces as those look whom a look must last a long time.

They didn't even say good-bye, for, if they were never to meet again, the look was not good-bye. And meet again it was not unlikely they would, for it had been already arranged that Isabel was to lead off the autumn entertainments; but the look did not mean that, either. As life had been planned for them, all subsequent meetings must be merely trivialities. They had met once, and fate had decided that they must never meet like that again. In that long look each knew that they met and parted for ever, autumn arrangements notwithstanding.

Each came out of that look as out of a great cathedral, and from that moment till the train left Theophil, with an unwonted sense of loneliness, by Jenny's side, they entered that cathedral no more. Their devotions were done for that day, and they must resume their secular duties, rippling idly over the great deeps of themselves.

One always leaves a station from which a dear friend has just gone with a certain subdued air, a certain bereaved hush in the voice, and even Jenny felt a momentary loneliness too. But it was not long before the doors of home opened again for her in the sound of Theophil's voice; and in the sense of the old familiar nearness to him she was back again safe in the only world she ever wished to dwell in.

It was more of an effort with Theophil, and the voice that made home for Jenny had a strange sound in his own ears, as though it were still talking to Isabel; but the effort was soon made, and though Jenny teased him a little and said she believed he had quite lost his, that was to say *her*, heart to Isabel, of course she believed no such thing. Doubt is too terrible a toy for true love to play with. You only dare to doubt as you must sometimes face the fear of death.

"I wish next October were here," said Jenny, artlessly; "it seems such a long time to wait to see her again."

Did Theophil wish the same? He hardly knew.

"Distance is such a silly thing," went on Jenny. "It seems to have been invented just to separate those who want to be together. It seems so arbitrary, so unnecessary."

"I suppose death is a form of distance," said Theophil, irrelevantly.

"Life too, I'm afraid," said Jenny.

"Yes, indeed, life too," assented Theophil, dreamily.

"If I were to die," said Jenny, suddenly, "would you still do what we said?"

"Why do you ask that, dear? You're a very serious little woman this morning. Of course I would. You know. But why do you ask me now?"

"Oh, only, dear, because I wonder whether we really ought to. Somehow Isabel's visit has made me feel that life is a bigger, fuller thing than I had dreamed, and that men like you, at all events, have duties towards it even greater than your love for a little thing like me."

"Jenny dear, don't talk like that. Why should you? You don't surely doubt my love!"

"Of course not, Theophil. It was only my silly little brain thinking for once in a while, — and I don't mean to be unkind, but really I rather mean it. Are you still quite sure there is nothing in the world more important than love?"

"Quite sure," he answered; "surer than ever — if that were possible. You are not beginning to doubt that? Certainly it is a silly little brain, if that's what its thinking is coming to."

"I don't mean it for myself. Little women have nothing but love to think of; but great men, men with a mission in the world . . ."

"Please, Jenny!"

"Well, dear, I mean it; and I sometimes think that perhaps, perhaps, I'm hindering your life; that if you were to be bothered with love at all, you should have married some clever, wonderful woman, — a woman, say, like Isabel."

"Jenny!"

"Of course, dear, I know you don't

think so," she continued; and he realised that it was all artless accident on her part—"Still I cannot help thinking it for you sometimes, dear, and sometimes I feel very selfish to have your love,—as though, so to say, I was wearing some-one else's crown."

"Jenny dear, will you promise never to talk like that again? A clever woman! To be a woman is to be a genius, but to be a clever woman is to be another man of talent."

"That would n't be fair to Isabel."

"No," assented Theophil, "Isabel is different too."

And that brought them to Theophil's office and good-bye till the evening.

For the evening there had been fixed an important church meeting, the first annual business meeting of minister and deacons since Londonderry had come to New Zion. It was an occasion of jubilation all round, particularly for Mr. Moggridge, who gave voice to New Zion's general satisfaction, you may be sure, in no uncertain terms of praise.

New Zion was, indeed, *New* Zion once more, he said, thanks to their indefatigable young pastor, — a play on words which was received with the applause due to so unmistakable a union of wit and truth.

Nor did the proceedings result in mere compliments. The church found itself rich enough to increase its minister's stipend; and when Theophil took Mr. Moggridge back to supper, another surprise awaited him, in the form of a suspicious-looking letter, which, being opened, revealed a quite unexceptionable £50 note, enclosed in a sheet of notepaper, on which was written — "From never mind who."

The writing was unknown to Londonderry, but there could be only one culprit.

"Of course, Mr. Moggridge, this is from you. Really . . ."

"No, sir, indeed; you make a mistake

there," protested Moggridge, lying badly, and growing purple.

"Who do *you* suspect, Jenny?"

"Why, of course, it's Mr. Moggridge!"

"Mr. Moggridge!" exclaimed Jenny impulsively, throwing her arms round Mr. Moggridge's surprised shoulders, and kissing him somewhere in his whiskers, — "Mr. Moggridge! you are the dearest, kindest man in the world!"

And Jenny was not far wrong.

"Mr. Londonderry," said Mr. Moggridge, by way of changing the subject, and warmly grasping the young man's hand, "New Zion's proud of you, sir — and so is Eli Moggridge."

And that moment would have been as good for all three, even without the fifty-pound note.

ZION CHAPEL 107

CHAPTER XIV

THE GREAT EVENT OF MR. TALBOT'S LIFE

I REALISE that any attempt henceforth to enchain the reader's interest with church meetings, or the like enthralments, will be more than hopeless. That is the worst of allowing love to creep into one's story. He insists on having the stage to himself, and in that determination the audience is entirely with him. Previously you may have been interested in all kinds of peaceable, unexciting things, far more good for you, but enter love, and all the rest is suddenly fallen tame beyond endurance.

It is of no use to urge that life's bill of the play includes many hardly less brilliant and attractive performers. They are all well enough in their way, till the eternal Paganini is there with his old fiddle once more at his shoulder; then there is an end of all seriousness, or a beginning, as you please.

Well, I'll do my best to get over the six months between March and October as quickly as possible; and, indeed, it will not be very difficult, after all, for very little happened, to speak of, during that time to any of the chief actors engaged in making this history.

Perhaps it was this consideration that prompted old Mr. Talbot — O, bother old Mr. Talbot! — that prompted old Mr. Talbot, I say, to take the important step of dying, when, poor old man! his death would give the least possible trouble.

There seemed as little reason for his dying as there had seemed for his living, for as far as anyone knew there was nothing the matter with him, except an extreme sleepiness of an evening, which was but natural in an old weary man who still kept at his stone-masonry though he was full seventy.

Night after night, for some weeks, he had been getting sleepier and sleepier.

"Why, dad, I never saw such an old sleepy-head" — his wife had rallied him good-naturedly one night, looking at him with a sudden odd expression in her face.

"Eh, lass, but I was noddin' and no mistake," said the old man, struggling drowsily with the heaviness, and presently succumbing once more.

"He's off again," said Mrs. Talbot to herself, as she lifted the lid of a pent saucepan in which some boiled onions were mightily bubbling in a wild little world of steam.

Presently the old man sighed deeply, — so you would have thought; but Mrs. Talbot, hurrying to him, knew that he had tried to say "Jane," and had said it for the last time.

Yes, he had been getting sleepier and sleepier; all his life he had been trying to sleep, and at last he slept.

To most people Mr. Talbot's death was

the first intimation of his ever having lived, and one rather resents for the old man the one day's publicity which death enforced upon him. It was indeed well for him that he was dead, for such unwonted excitement would surely have killed him. This important coming and going of undertakers; this populous invasion of friends talking like muffled drums in the front parlour, and passing up and down and up and down the stairs, in and out and in and out of his still room; this throng of neighbours awaiting him in the streets; these plumed impatient horses, and these carriages of dark grandeur— "Jane, why ever did n't you bury me by the back door?" would surely have been the old man's pitiful complaint could he have known.

However, the day passed and the old man was safe at last, where no front-parlour visitors should affright him more, and where no one would trouble his old brains for speech any more; and to all, save one, his death was but as though he had moved a little farther into the kitchen.

It seemed almost strange that even his wife should miss him. One had thought so little of them as man and wife. One could hardly, even by process of thinking, realise that between these rinded and wrinkled beings love had once hung like a rosy cloud, from which one day had sprung Jenny.

On one or two occasions, indeed, they had been surprised in an uncanny semblance of a caress, and once in a while an almost supernatural retrospect had lit up and vanished again in an unaccustomed tender word; and to have been present then was to feel somehow frightened.

Ah! the gay young leaves no longer kiss across in the morning sun, but the stern old trees have meetings you know not of far beneath the ground. Their roots are twisted and twined in a wonderful embrace there; there in the dark they are very close together, and shall not be wrenched apart without groanings that cannot be uttered.

Jenny can hardly be said to have missed her father, except through her mother, who seemed suddenly to grow a little deafer, a little more dim-sighted, just a trifle less brisk and busy than before, and with a touch about her of that old-age awesomeness that mutters to itself in corners and seems to know strange things.

Yes, Jane missed her John. Her old heart knew that he was no longer sitting in the kitchen.

CHAPTER XV

JENNY'S BOTTOM DRAWER

JENNY and her old mother began to grow closer to each other at this time. Perhaps it was because the old woman felt lonelier, and perhaps, too, because the loss of her old man had sent her thoughts wandering among the enchanted fields of her young days, that she began to talk sometimes to Jenny about her marriage, and to give her quaint advice on the subject of "managing" husbands; "as if," Jenny smilingly said to herself, "an old man like father was the same, belonged even to the same race, as Theophil."

Perhaps Mrs. Talbot scented some such reflection in Jenny's expression; at all events, she answered it with an "Eh, but all men are alike, my dear, under their skins, — all alike, and they need humouring and managing just in the same way, prince or peasant."

The idea of "managing" Theophil had something repulsive in it for Jenny; there was an element of deceit, of cunning, implied which didn't go with her ideas of true love and the life beautiful of which she was dreaming. She didn't believe that men and women who loved were really different from each other, and perhaps she was right.

About this time, too, Mrs. Talbot began to produce from mysterious treasure-caves, entered apparently from an old press in her bedroom, all kinds of wonderful things which would be useful to Jenny some day in her house: terrible little ornaments, — very sacred, though, — sad quaintnesses of the spirit of beauty pathetically fumbling about in country brains; wool mats worked in the primary colours; and such wool wonders as a wool basket of flowers, in which real wool flowers grew out of a wool basket which you held by an over-arching wool handle, the whole worked with undeniable but how forlorn ingenuity, — a prehistoric relic of Mrs. Talbot's legendary school-days: survivals from a period which is best summed up in the one wonderful word "antimacassar," a period when for some unrecorded reason men and women had to protect their furniture against their oleaginous selves, and beautiful locks were guarded from lover's fingers by coats of triple oil.

But these were things worth having, too, — bits of old lace and prim embroidery, that bore the stamp of a refinement that is never old-fashioned; and when Mrs. Talbot descended from the beautiful she could show you real treasures.

I don't think there was any word in the language, not even Bible words, which Mrs. Talbot pronounced with such an accent of solemnity as the word "linen." The words "China" and "cut glass," and perhaps "silver," ran it close, but "linen" was undoubtedly the word in which all Mrs. Talbot's sense of the seriousness of living, her sense of household distinction, her deep sense of the importance of prosperity, and her stern love of cleanliness found most impressive utterance.

Mrs. Talbot could never have smiled as she said "linen."

And the linen she had been storing for Jenny might indeed have been the very stuff of which lilies are made, lilies smelling of lavender.

Such pairs of sheets! A queen might even fear to await her lord lying amid such linen; for white indeed must be the body that dares rivalry with Mrs. Talbot's sheets, — sheets which might indeed be said to settle that old question of the snows of yester-year.

Mais ou sont les neiges d'antan?

Surely they have been settling, flake on flake, year after year, in Mrs. Talbot's linen-press, till at last there is quite a snowdrift of fair white linen for Jenny and Theophil to lie in.

Yes! another six months and Christmas will be here; and, after Christmas is turned, the weeks till February the 12th — the second anniversary of Theophil's coming to New Zion — will fly by in no time.

Meanwhile Mrs. Talbot and Jenny — with occasional contributions from Theophil — began to busy themselves with Jenny's bottom drawer.

Translated into the language of those more magnificent circles in which this simple-hearted romance has no desire to move, a "bottom drawer" might be described as a trousseau, though such translation would be only partially correct. A bottom drawer is a good deal more than a trousseau. It is the corner of a girl's wardrobe, usually its bottom drawer, where the home that is to be begins to take shape in deposits of various kissed objects, minor articles of apparel, of ornament or use, — handkerchiefs such as we have already seen Jenny marking, in defiance of the old prophecy that the bride who dares even to write her married name before her marriage will never know a wedding day; quaint candlesticks that had to be picked up in some old curiosity shop as come upon or be missed altogether; pretty shoes of a pattern you were n't likely to meet with again; occasionally, perhaps, even an anticipatory wedding present, that some friend who would be far away in Australia when the day came had already contributed; a pretty tea-service Theophil had suddenly taken a fancy to buy for Jenny one day, — "any straw will help a nest;" a sweet and rather naughty picture that must never be hung anywhere but in their little sacred bedroom, — "O love, our little room!"

How often did Jenny bend lovingly over that drawer, which by now had spread itself over a whole chest of drawers, — for home was growing, growing, — only a few more months and it would have grown so big and real that nothing but a little house would hold it. And Theophil was brought sometimes to peep in too, — "O love, think of it — our little home."

CHAPTER XVI

THEOPHIL ALL THIS TIME

HAVE I seemed to shirk the subject of Theophil's feelings all this time? Well, I confess I have rather shrunk from writing down in so many words that he was in love with Isabel, — obvious as the fact has been, — just as he himself shrank from admitting the same truth even to his own soul.

When he had sat up in his study that night of the recital, he had looked the whole sad splendid truth in its wonderful face, had loved it wildly for an hour, and then shut his eyes to it for ever.

He knew that Isabel was the woman God had made for him, sweet, dear Jenny the woman he had made for himself, and he bowed before the work of the greater artist.

Never voice nor look nor touch of woman had affected Theophil before as the least tone or glance or movement of Isabel stirred him to the centre of his being. To meet her eyes was to release a music that went shuddering through the whole world; her lightest word was filled with echoes of infinite things. Not a lover only, but anyone with instincts for such perceptions, looking at Isabel, would have said: There is a woman who is needed to make some man a great poet, a great artist, some kind of great man! She belongs to the history-making women. Hundreds of women will attract men by the hundred where she will attract comparatively few, but that few will be the pick of men; and some day, when the other women have gone the way of all sweet roses, she will still remain (if she has found an artist to understand her face) the frontispiece of some distinguished biography, or hang in a gallery of the period among the few faces that were indestructibly personal; not the faces that have lived, but the faces that still go on living, the faces that are influences still, the unique, dæmonic faces.

Isabel was indeed a muse that waited for her poet. The mere idea of such a woman, cherished across dividing seas and separating years, will help a man be great. To grow great near or far is the one way to be hers, and to pile up great work for her sake is perhaps the best way to love her. She could never be his wife, but she might still be his muse, resolved Theophil, feigning in that reflection for the moment a more human comfort than, alas! there really was.

But was there to be no loss to Jenny in this?

> "True love in this differs from gold or clay,
> That to divide is not to take away."

It is the convenient old plea of the poets, and yet it is sometimes true. It was true here. There is, I know, a sort of primitive man or woman — I believe they will some day be exhibited in menageries — who cannot be on with a new love without being ungratefully off with the old. All depends of what the two loves are made. If it is bodily fire and no more, of course the new love will put out the old as the great sun puts out a little smouldering fire; and the majority of so-called love-stories are merely disastrous conflagrations of that sort. In such cases the new love is no sooner found than the old becomes grievous, a burden; by a malignant witchcraft the old charms have grown veritably repellent, and "all the heaven that was" irretrievably disenchanted. Which is the illusion, one wonders, — the original enchantment or the final disenchantment?

When, however, love can give a better account of its preferences than this, and point out, say in Jenny, many good reasons why she was at first and must for ever remain love-worthy, whatever rival reasons for love another woman may bring; when too there is added to those reasons for loving Jenny the dear habit of loving her, the gratitude — love must forgive the word — which has accumulated interest upon the original love, the beauties that have been gained by becoming familiarities, and the familiarities that have become beauties by very use, — well, really, is it such a hardship, after all, for a man to be expected to keep true to his Jenny?

Oh! but passion does n't reason like this. Indeed, O passionate reader! Is passion, then, merely a wild beast, a savage, a blind fire? Must it forfeit its fine name if it remembers mercy or owns duty? Is it any less passion because it refuses sometimes to glut itself, and dares to go hungry all its days instead; any less passion because it chooses to burn up its own heart in an agony of its own consuming fire?

Mere violence is not a strength but a weakness in passion, and sometimes there is more passion in patience than in anything else in the world. A passion that knows not pity is merely a dæmonic possession, and should be taken to the madhouse.

I confess that there is nothing in the world more amazing to me than the easy brutality with which one hears of some men doing what is called "breaking off their engagements." Only a new face has to show itself, and the old face at once disappears with a blow and a wail.

Murder, of course, is one way out of many difficult situations, and the worst kinds of murder are by no means capital offences. It is true that all engagements are not made by the same vital bonds as that of Jenny's and Theophil's, but many are. For a man wilfully to break an engagement means sometimes that the whole love-life in a woman is atrophied, all that made her woman stabbed to the quick of life.

Yet no one who knows anything of

women can have failed to remark that women themselves are even more brutal in this matter. Nothing could exceed the executioner-like promptitude with which a woman will despatch a man for whom she has ceased to care. But in her case there is to be urged that, though fundamentally love is of equal importance to man and woman, it does not so often mean the absolute saving or wrecking of a man's life as it does a woman's. It is not a disgrace to a man to be jilted; it is to a woman. For a woman to be jilted is for her to have failed, — as a woman; and for a woman to have failed as a woman is for her to value no other success.

All this to maintain, in spite of the reader, that Londonderry is no milksop because he is not going to jilt — that is, murder — poor little Jenny, throw up New Zion, and seek his new love on the wild winds. But the agony of it none the less! O Jenny! Jenny! sweet and true and good and dear as ever, — if only you would just take a sudden fancy for someone else!

Meanwhile the months were going by, and the day drawing nearer when, for a brief moment of fire, the orbits of those two separated lives were to touch once more.

What of Isabel during these months? The woman whom God had created for Theophilus Londonderry did not forget her promise to write to the woman whom Theophilus Londonderry had created in his own image. Wonderful letters, of course! Why don't women publish volumes of their letters, as men collect their scattered essays? There is no writing in the world more immediately, conqueringly personal than a really clever woman's letters; and they are not always compromising.

Isabel's letters were the perfection of self-expression. Her handwriting swept across the page just as she would walk down a street, at once eager and yet stately and subtle-rhythmed; the shape of some of the words reminded you of her hats, — hats everyone thought she paid guineas for, but which she made for herself at a cost perhaps of five shillings: hats which were Paris with a touch of fairyland, somewhere an unobtrusive feather of the fantastic, somewhere a personal magic in the inimitable twist or lie of a bow —; her face looked out at you from a g or an x, a gesture flashed back to you in a sudden distinguished stroke of the pen, and her voice was somewhere, everywhere, among the words, like a violin.

Without any apparent literary device she contrived to make you, while you read her letters, do what she was doing, see what she was seeing, and form, as though acted on by some magic property in the words, pictures of all she told you.

One piece of news you would not expect her to have told. I have said that women are both executioners of the tiresome. In this Isabel, I fear, was no exception to her sex. Like most independent girls in London, she had a little theatre-guard of devoted men friends, who took it in turn to companion her to plays or picture-galleries; and these, with admirable tact, she contrived to keep in, to them, the unsatisfactory relation of brothers. One of these, however, had of late been growing dangerously unfraternal. His presents had been growing expensive. Cigarettes and chocolates, and pretty editions, like gloves, and boxes of flowers, are every pretty woman's lawful spoils; but costlier gifts are to be looked on with suspicion. Besides, the doomed man's letters had been growing warmer. Indeed, Isabel remembered with something like a shudder, so soon as she was back in her little room, with its curious pictures and its general sense of exotic refinement, that she had allowed him to kiss her the last time they had been together. The reminiscence decided her. Theophil could never be hers; but at least no facile or mediocre attachments should fill his place. So at once there is posted a letter, as kind as cruelty can make it, and with it go a little ormolu clock, a pair of mother-of-pearl opera-glasses, a lovely fan it was hard, Isabel, to part with, — and there is an end of that.

"Not after Theophil!" she sighed, as she took up her great Persian cat, and, like it, sat gazing into the fire that flickered dreamily among her fantastic possessions, — a mystery gazing idly into a mystery.

CHAPTER XVII

"O THAT 'T WERE POSSIBLE . . ."

WELL, the months have at last gone by, —dark solid bodies of absence, not a day mercifully lost count of by the old calendar-maker, not an hour of the long sentence remitted for a brave patience in the waiting. They are reckoning by weeks at last, and now, excitedly, by days, breathlessly now by little fast-dispersing hours.

The blackness that filled the world was a month ago streaked with gray; three weeks ago there was a line of faint colour in the east; a fortnight, and there are scarlet plumes in the far heaven, and a faint twitter of song; a week, and the whole sky is a commotion of glory and birds.

To meet again! O to meet again, just to look at each other again! We are philosophers, we are brave, we shall remember Jenny, but O! the rapture of just beholding each other again.

"Thank God, you are alive! you are real! O Theophil, there is the little scar on your forehead I've been longing to see."

"Yes! it is Isabel! She walks just as she did a thousand years ago. I am carrying her rugs. How well I remember her umbrella!"

"How fantastic absence is!" said Isabel, as the three friends sat once more that evening in the little study where nothing seemed to have changed, and where they seemed to have been sitting all the hours of those now quite disrespectfully forgotten months.

"Yes, but how real!" said Jenny. It was Jenny who said "how real!"

How fantastic, too, is the present! Sometimes, perhaps nearly always, it tortures us with the unreality, the unrealisability of precious moments that are flying, flying, and can never come again; and at other times it equally eludes us with a sense of their indestructibility. To-night the present had chosen to seem real. Theophil felt, as he looked at Isabel, that this wonderful nearness could never pass away. Her dress, her coiled *cendré* hair, her soft smile, her very attitudes, seemed to wear a curious expression of everlastingness. Yes, she would sit just like that, and he and Jenny would sit near her for ever and ever. No mere abstractions like Time and Space could fill with emptiness the place where she now sat and smiled. In some mystical way eternity had breathed upon this hour and given it immortality. It had been suddenly touched with a wand into an enchanted permanence. Theosophists tell of an astral light, where every moment of time endures in strange paintings upon space. Isabel and Theophil and Jenny were sitting together in the astral light.

And yet the hours had already been flying, for the recital was already over, — New Zion more in love with Isabel than ever. The same little supper as six months ago had been merry and come to an end, the guests had gone, the house was quiet, and this hour that seemed so real was the frail last of that day of dreams.

Yes! but an arrangement had been made which perhaps accounts for the security of that hour. Isabel's agents had planned for her a little circular tour in northern towns comparatively adjacent to Coalchester, and when a fortnight of such recitals was ended, she was to return and give still another recital at New Zion. Then there must be parting, real black parting again. Meanwhile, the fortnight that lay between the two days of meeting gained a curious sense of being really spent together. As two walking together on a long road may separate, and one walk till almost out of sight of the other and then slowly return, but the two endure no sense of parting, feeling together all the time, so Isabel and Theophil felt about this fortnight.

But did they speak no word, look no look all these hours, of all their hearts cried out to say? Was Jenny there all the time? Nearly. Still there was a moment granted them, which, added to the two moments previously recorded, made a total perhaps of four minutes, which life so far generously allowed them to be alone together in. Yet such is love's miraculous velocity that it had said all it needed to say, given all, in those four minutes. All it had to say to-night was just two Christian names, said so solemnly, so tenderly, so honestly. Just "Isabel," just "Theophil," and a long quiet clasp of hand and eyes. It was enough. It is written.

CHAPTER XVIII

ONE DAY OUT OF ALL THE YEARS

IT was not enough!
If you would safely renounce a joy, you had best enjoy something of it first. Renunciation must have something to live on. You can "take up the whole of love and utter it," and *then* "say adieu for ever," but not before.

I have asked mercy for Jenny, though it was perhaps hardly necessary, for the world always pities Jenny. Now I would ask it for Isabel and Theophil, who are thus quietly to sacrifice the greatest thing in their lives, the one reality for which they have come into existence, for Jenny's sake. Great is their love for each other, but even greater and stranger must be their involuntary love for an invisible goodness, an ideal of ineffable pity. They are going to die that Jenny may live.

Strange, this gentle heroism of human creatures one for the other. Would it be unfair to ask that each should support the anguish of his own destiny, and that when Jenny's turn has come she should take her lightning? Hers, had she known it, was the cup of anguish here; for Theophil and Isabel had been decreed the cup of joy. But will they drink it? No, they will change the cups; perhaps the bitter cup will grow sweet near the dregs, being drunk together.

Yet this love of theirs, this perilous chance for Jenny, was none of their making. Their joy had been given to them by unseen hands. It is fairly theirs. Next time, perhaps, it will be their turn to suffer. It is Jenny's now . . .

But no! the good heart of humanity will defeat the cruel ruling of the gods. Let the lightning come upon them — not little Jenny.

Yet for this, Jenny, you will not grudge them their piteous reward. Yours are all the years, Jenny. You will spare them one day out of all the years. Think, Jenny, of the hours and hours and hours you and Theophil have spent in careless happiness, and they — one almost laughs to think of it — have just so far been granted four minutes. For four minutes out of infinite time life has privileged them to be alone together.

It will be far safer too. Otherwise you know not with what fearful flame love will fill the chasms under ground, circling and seething in the fiery darkness. Theophil loves you, but some day your home will suddenly be rent from cope to base, unless his poor heart may speak, yea, babble itself, just once in Isabel's ears.

A temptation had come to Theophil. At first he put it aside. Then passion, wiser for once than reason, told him that it was a necessity, and he knew that passion was right. A week of the fortnight had gone, and Theophil remembered that Isabel would now be in the neighbourhood of certain famous woods where in his boyhood he had often wandered, and he remembered that she was to have the Monday quite free. That Monday they should spend together in those enchanted woods. His secular business often took him to towns thirty or forty miles away, and it was not startling for him not to return till late at night. Thus Isabel and he should steal their one day out of all the years.

So there went a note without one word of love in it to tell Isabel that love was coming by the morning train; and so on that morning Isabel stood waiting for love at that little wayside station, and presently, with a mighty rushing sound of iron and brass, love came and stood very quietly by her side, and looked into her eyes.

They took each other's hands quietly, and left the station without a word; nor did they speak for a long while, walking blissfully side by side through a village street which was to take them to the green and lonely woods. Soon the houses were passed, and they still walked on silent, listening to the song of their nearness.

Now, as they drank each other's presence through every feasting nerve, they knew how starved they had been. As the lane narrowed and gloomed green, dipping through caverns of bright leaves, they drew closer, and smiled gently on each other; but they were not going to speak for a long while yet. Had they not come away into this loneliness that they might be silent together, that they might sit, hour after hour, and just watch each other, lost in an ecstasy of contemplation, a trance of recognition, a fascination that was almost fearful, that was so kind and yet so cruel in its very power?

The woods are very still, but there is nothing in the world so still as these two lovers, as they lie down on the green earth and gaze on each other, hour after hour.

When they find a word as great as their silence, they will speak it — but they will find none except it be "Isabel," except it be "Theophil."

And great passion has as little use for caresses as for words, and kisses, which gay sensual love gathers greedily like little golden flowers, and pays for nimbly with little, pretty words, will be almost as rare as words.

Kisses! it is not to eat bonbons that these two have come out into the woods.

Kisses! what kiss of the blind lips could match the kiss of those rapt tragic eyes!

Kisses are but the diminutives of the great word "love;" they are but the small change of passion, meteorites, star-dust of the great and terrible planet.

Their souls are swung high above time and space in one never-ending kiss, — the kiss of that predestined irrefragable union, of which meetings and partings and kisses and caresses and words, and every other fragmentary mode of expression, are but trivial accidents, to which distance is still nearness, and nearness is still distance.

Their love is a property of eternal elements. It is fated as the union of magnetic powers, it obeys chemic laws of irresistible combination. They are Isabel and Theophil, — that is their love; they are in the world together, — that is their marriage.

But passion will not be all day a tragedian. He has many moods. He is a great wit, — how bright, how bright, he makes the brain! — a merry comrade, a little, tender, silly child; and these two sad ones laughed together, too, in the still woods, — for was not the most exquisite humourist in the world their companion, love, who is all things by turns, and all things wise?

And they feasted together, wine and great grapes, spread out on the earth's green table; and they called each other silly, beautiful names, and they feigned sad little glad stories — and called the wood their home: this was their breakfast-oak, and that glade should be their great hall, and high, high up in yonder beech, where the squirrel was sitting, should be their secret little bed-chamber, hung in blue and green, with a ceiling of stars. They should climb it each night on a ladder of moonlight, and slide down from it each morning on the first strong rays of the sun. And sometimes if it frightened them with being too near heaven, they would seek out a dell of fine moss and creep close together into the arms of the kind earth-mother, and then sleep while the stars kept watch.

O, yes, it would be a wonderful life together.

Then suddenly the child's play would cease, as the birds stop singing with the coming of the stars, and silence would sweep over them again, and a great kiss would leap out of the silence, like a flame that lights up heaven from north to south, and they would hang together, lost in an anguish of desire.

The setting sun was turning the wood into halls of strange light, and spreading golden couches here and there in its deep recesses.

"Theophil . . ." sighed Isabel.

"Wife . . ." sighed Theophil — (ah! Jenny!) and then a voice that seemed to be neither's, and yet seemed to be the voice of both, — a voice like a dove smothered in sweetness between their breasts, — said, "Let us go deeper into the wood."

Later, when the stars had come, two white faces came glimmering from the innermost chancel of the wood's green darkness. They passed close together, still as phantoms among the trees, and when they came out on to the lane they stood still.

"Theophil," said one voice, "if I should be dying, and I should send for you, will you promise me to come?"

"Isabel," said another voice, "if I should be dying, and I should send for you, will you promise *me* to come?"

And each voice vowed to the other, and said, "I would come, and I would go with you."

And all these words had once been Jenny's, but they had been Isabel's first.

CHAPTER XIX

PREPARATIONS FOR A FAST AND OTHER SADNESS

As the sharing of a cruel or unworthy secret must be the most terrible of all human relationships, the sharing of a beautiful secret is the most blest. Thus, for the week following this day of days, Theophil and Isabel went about their daily lives with all heaven in their hearts, and, divided though they were, possessed by a mystical certitude of inner union which they felt no extension of space or endurance of time could destroy.

Such a marriage as theirs is, of course, the dream of all separated lovers, "the love that waited and in waiting died" the theme of many poets; and there have been great historic love-stories to prove such love a possibility of human hearts;

yet, alas! for the experiment that must so often fail, for the weak wills of loving that will so truly and yet must loose their holds, — the fire that promised itself food in memory for a thousand years, but needs the sensual fuel of sight and touch after all; the love that believed it could go on trusting through centuries of silence, yet dies at last of little earthly doubts!

For this tremendous fast which you are to make believe a feast, trust in each other is the one condition that may avail. This trust must come of no mere exchange of vow or deeply-sworn and eloquent promise; it must be knowledge one heart of the other, clear and absolute; and such knowledge in your short hour of revelation you must have learned so passionately that, like poetry learnt in childhood, it is henceforth no longer a forgettable, detachable part of your mind's furniture, but a well-spring of instinct for ever. Is your lady true? You will ask that only when you ask: Is she beautiful?

ZION CHAPEL

Such confidence as this is comparatively common in friendship, but it is very rare in love: whether it was to be justified in the case of Isabel and Theophil, time alone could show. Meanwhile they felt calm and happy, as only two can feel who have discovered in each other the one unchanging reality in a world of flowing shadow.

It was very wonderful, in quite a new way, to meet again. Their love was no longer hunger and unrest, it had gained the impassioned peace of great accepted realities. It was married love now. As the quiet firm hands held each other again, there seemed to be long retrospects of tried and tender intercourse in their very touch. Their eyes held a past in them as well as a future. There was no hurry of the emotions now, no reason for haste in the seeking and giving of tenderness, no need to snatch and clutch the good gifts of love as though there was but a short day for the giving.

Their love had grown conscious of its eternity.

It held but one lasting sadness, — that it might not be revealed to Jenny. So little did they regard their love as one essentially for concealment, that the temptation to include Jenny in their bond was at moments a danger. It was so beautiful, and actually, though unconsciously, she was so integral a part of its beauty.

Theirs was that dream of a threefold union, in which, so to say, jealousy shall be so taken into the confidence of, so held to the heart of, love, that it shall transform itself into love too; and, from being the lonely tragic third, become, as the other two, one of an indivisible trinity. Such unions of natures of especial grace have been born under like conditions of fated intercourse, and they have been unions of a strange beauty, the more blest by the sense of a conquest over love's one unworthiness, its egoism. As the *égoisme à deux* is finer than an

ZION CHAPEL

egoism of one, so this *égoisme à trois*, if you will, is again finer by its additional inclusiveness.

Perhaps it had proved wiser in the end to yield to this temptation too. But the tragic risk was one to dismay experiment. The strength of such a union is literally the strength of its weakest link. Jenny loved both Isabel and Theophil, and both Isabel and Theophil loved Jenny; and in the love of the two girls, there was an element of affection that was more impassioned than friendship. Jenny indeed loved Isabel so much that it might well have proved that her love, with nothing but gladness, could have added its volume to Theophil's, and the three loves, meeting in one river of love, flowed on together to the eternal sea.

But the tragic risk! The alternative was — heart-break, death. They had vowed to save Jenny from the lightning. Perhaps it would not destroy, but only transfigure, after all, — yet the test was lightning; and for whom that we love dare we venture such an ordeal, though it were to win them Paradise?

No! Jenny must never know. And yet, perhaps, if Jenny had been told . . . Well, the greatest love for another cannot guard all the gates of chance. And, alas! these two, loyal as they were, for one unguarded moment were to leave open a gate of their Paradise, — when we withdraw into Paradise we should see that all the gates are closed, — and Jenny, by a like chance, was to take into her soul one blinding glimpse of them there.

It was the evening of the last recital, and Theophil and Isabel had gone down to "Zion" a few minutes before the hour arranged, Jenny, who for some trivial reason was detained, to meet them at the hall. An audience was already gathered there; but this Theophil and Isabel avoided, entering the building by the minister's private entrance into his vestry, which communicated by a dark staircase with the chapel and the lecture-hall where the recital was to be given. There was a light in the vestry, but no one was there, though they might have expected Mr. Moggridge. For a moment, to their eternal sorrow, they forgot all but that they were once more alone and together; and as they sought each other's arms, standing in the centre of that grim little room, a weak anguish came over Theophil, and he exclaimed, —

"Oh, Isabel, to think that I have lost you! lost you!"

But Isabel was stronger: "No, dear, you have not lost, you have found me. To have lost each other would have been never to have met. Dear, I love to think that you might be weak for my sake. No woman can help a man be strong who cannot first make him weak. Ah, love, how weak I could be for your sake, — and how strong! . . . but be strong for mine, be strong for Jenny's sake. I love that best."

Then for a moment they stood lost once more, locked in an embrace so touchingly kind, so sheltering, so calm, that their very attitude was home; and, had they had ears or eyes for a world outside that home, they might have seen, at that dark half-opened staircase door, a little face look in happy and draw back dead; for Jenny had followed them more quickly than she or they had expected, and, not finding them in the lecture-hall, had sought them here with a light heart. She had heard none of their words; she had only seen that look of home upon their faces and written across their arms.

Very quietly she stole away. She felt very dazed and tired. The shock had been so swift that already it seemed half unreal. She felt she must sit down, and, passing into the silent chapel, lit only with dim reflections from without, she sank on to a seat and thought of little but that it was good to be sitting down, and that the darkness was good, and that there looming out of the shadow was Theophil's pulpit, and beneath was her little harmonium, — to-morrow night would be her choir-practice, she must n't forget that; no, she must n't forget that — and then the darkness began to frame flashing pictures of that dreadful glimpse of brightness — were they still standing like that? — how happy they looked! — and would they always go on standing together in brightness like that, while she sat here in the darkness. Well, the darkness was good; how she should dread brightness for the future. If only she need not go to the recital! — might she not be spared that? No! she must have courage, she must go, they must not know she had seen them, not yet, not till she had thought what must be done, not till she had made her plans. It would have to be talked of if she let them know. That would be terrible. Isabel would be gone to-morrow, and then she might speak to Theophil, might set him free. But now she must go, — she must not be later than they; they would be passing down to the hall presently, she must be there before them, — she must be quick, — she must go now. . . .

As Isabel and Theophil entered the hall together, and smiled a recognising smile at Jenny already in her place, she was able to smile back at them, though there were some who thought she looked very white, and found her very quiet when they tried to talk to her.

She couldn't help remarking to herself how little of the common resentment she felt towards the two on whose faces she now saw a happiness which she wondered she had not seen before. But her anguish was too great for resentment. She felt towards their love as she might have felt towards death, — it was a terrible fact, and in her good heart there was already the beginning of pity for them too. Perhaps she felt that it was a little unkind of them not to have trusted her, — just as a child might who had felt worthy of our trust, but had been deemed too young to share it. If they had only told her, might she not have loved their love? (Ah! if we would only trust the deeps in those we love!)

Had Isabel only seen that white face in the dark doorway, she would have spared Jenny one of her recitations that night. It was a poem of Mrs. Browning's, perhaps the most poignant poem of renunciation ever written, and Isabel had chosen it, as love will choose a song, for the fearful joy of singing it where all may hear but one only may understand. It was the poem of a like renunciation to theirs, though for different reasons; but there was sufficient literal application to them for Jenny now to understand it too. It was called a "Denial," and began:—

"We have met late—it is too late to meet,
   O friend, not more than friend!
Death's forecome shroud is tangled round my
   feet,
And if I step or stir, I touch the end.

In this last jeopardy
Can I approach thee, — I, who cannot move?
How shall I answer thy request for love?
    Look in my face and see.

" I might have loved thee in some former days.
    Oh, then, my spirits had leapt
As now they sink, at hearing thy love-praise!
Before these faded cheeks were overwept,
    Had this been asked of me,
To love thee with my whole strong heart and head, —
I should have said still . . . Yes, but *smiled* and said,
    ' Look in my face and see!'

" But now . . . God sees me, God, who took my heart
    And drowned it in life's surge.
In all your wide warm earth I have no part —
A light song overcomes me like a dirge.
    Could love's great harmony
The saints keep step to when their bonds are loose,
Not weigh me down? am *I* a wife to choose?
    Look in my face and see —

" While I behold, as plain as one who dreams,
    Some woman of full worth,
Whose voice, as cadenced as a silver stream's,
Shall prove the fountain-soul which sends it forth

ZION CHAPEL

One younger, more thought-free
And fair and gay, than I, thou must forget,
With brighter eyes than these . . . which are
    not wet —
Look in my face and see!

" So farewell thou, whom I have known too late
    To let thee come so near.
Be counted happy while men call thee great,
And one beloved woman feels thee dear ! —
    Not I ! — that cannot be,
I am lost, I am changed, — I must go farther
    where
The change shall take me worse, and no one
    . dare
Look in my face and see."

The agony of this verse as one reads it is heartbreaking, but as Isabel recited it, it was unbearable, and others in that audience besides Jenny felt the personal cry in the voice, though none but Jenny knew its destination. But to Jenny's ears the exquisite wifeliness of the last verse was fuller of pain than all the rest, —

"Meantime I bless thee. By these thoughts of
    mine
    I bless thee from all such !
I bless thy lamp to oil, thy cup to wine,
Thy hearth to joy, thy hand to an equal touch

Of loyal troth. For me,
I love thee not, I love thee not! — away!
There 's no more courage in my soul to say
'Look in my face and see.' "

When Isabel sat down, amid hushed clapping, it was observed that Miss Jenny Talbot had fainted. Theophil sprang with others to her assistance, and Jenny, being carried into an ante-room for air and water, presently reviving, asked faintly for Mr. Moggridge to take her home, the thought of the big kind man coming into her mind with a sense of homely refuge.

"There, there," he said, "you 'll be better in a minute;" and when she was strong enough to walk, he took her home, Theophil, filled with sudden misgivings, having to see the evening's entertainment to its close.

Mr. Moggridge blamed the bad ventilation, as he tenderly helped Jenny along the few yards to home.

"No," said Jenny, with a big tearing

sigh, "I don't think it was that. It was that last poem, I think. It seemed so terrible to think of two people having to part like that; don't you think so, Mr. Moggridge?"

Mr. Moggridge did. "And then," he said, "Miss Strange has such a way of giving it out, it's almost more than human nature can bear."

"Yes; her voice," said Jenny, "seemed like a stream of tears."

When Theophil and Isabel returned from Zion, they seemed so full of real anxiety, as indeed they were, that Jenny's poor heart felt just a passing ray of warmth, a little less cast out into eternal loneliness. She gave the same explanation as to Mr. Moggridge, not significantly, but half intending a kind veiled message to them. "It seemed so terrible to think of two people having to part like that," she said again.

And presently she pleaded weariness to go to bed earlier than usual.

"But don't you hurry, Isabel," said Jenny. "You and Theophil will not see each other for a long time again."

"Sleep well," said Isabel, kissing her; and as she did so, she thought there was a curious convulsiveness in Jenny's embrace.

When she had gone, the two looked at each other. "She seemed strange," said Isabel.

"I think I will go and see her for a moment," said Theophil.

So it was that, tapping at Jenny's door, he found her lying across her bed with the gas still down. "Crying, dear!" he exclaimed.

"O Theophil dear, don't come," she said; "it's only silly nerves. Go back to Isabel; I shall be better when I've had a sleep. Do go, dear, like a kind boy. I'm better by myself. No . . . it is nothing, — nothing but nerves. Do go, dear. Good-night."

And with a foreboding heart Theophil

went back to Isabel. Yet, as Jenny had said, they were not to see each other for a long time again; and if presently Theophil forgot Jenny crying upstairs, was it not because he did not know the reason of her tears?

On the morrow Jenny pleaded weariness and stayed in bed, so that Theophil saw Isabel off to London alone, and he did not see Jenny again till the evening.

CHAPTER XX

IN WHICH JENNY CRIES

JENNY was not at the door that evening to welcome Theophil home, as she usually was, and she made some excuse not to join him at dinner; but at last, when the quiet secure hour which had always been theirs between dinner and bedtime had come, she came into his room quietly and sat in her accustomed chair.

She had been fighting all day to gain strength for this hour, and her will was bravely set to speak what must be spoken. But she must firmly choke back all the sweetness of the memories which sprang to her with kind eyes, as the familiar little room that had not changed opened its arms to her, alas! an ironical symbol of unchangeableness. One touch of tenderness too vivid and she would break down.

And here was Theophil rising from his desk and coming to her with true love in his eyes, as he had done so many, many happy nights.

Was it, after all, a dream — that terrible picture of two lighted figures that was for ever in her eyes? No, there was a voice that went day and night with the dream, a voice of terrible tenderness that kept crying: "Meantime I bless thee . . ." — "I bless thy lamp to oil, thy cup to wine ... ." Ah, no, it was real, real. The trial was not to pass from her in a dream.

Theophil had knelt down at her side and taken her hand gently and would have kissed her, but that her eyes were so full of pain as she turned them to meet his. Besides, strange words to hear! she was asking him not to kiss her.

"Theophil dear, don't kiss me yet. I have something to say, and if you kiss me I shall have no strength to say it."

"Jenny!"

"Dear," she began with a voice that

seemed to bleed at every word, "I want to be so kind. I don't want to hurt you with a single word. You'll believe that, won't you?"

Theophil pressed her hand for assent, but already in a flash the whole revelation was upon him. Jenny knew he loved Isabel. This awful pain that was all over her was the lightning from which they had willed to save her.

"Theophil," Jenny had gone on, and there seemed a death in every word, "I know that you love Isabel."

"O Jenny!"

"I saw you together, dear, in the vestry last night. It was an accident. You didn't hear me."

"O my Jenny! I would rather have died than this."

"Yes, I think you would, dear. But you must not be too sad. Life is terrible, — like this. I understand it now. I know it was not you, or Isabel, or me. It was just fate — and we must try and

ZION CHAPEL 165

help each other. Don't think I have been only sorry for myself. Don't think that of me. But I think you should have trusted me, dear."

"We longed to tell you," said Theophil, with his head bowed in distress in Jenny's lap, while she softly stroked his hair with an absent tenderness, though her eyes looked straight in front of her, and her voice was as if she were talking to herself.

"We longed to tell you," he repeated.

"O I wish you had."

"We feared it, dear."

"Yes, yes, I know. I was only a little child the day before yesterday. I have never been worthy to be your wife, dear. I have known it all the time. I should never have taken your love. It has never been mine. . . ."

"But . . ." she continued, "I will give it all back now. It is not too late. I have kept it pure . . . for Isabel. I can give it to her, darling, with a kind heart —for she is worthy. She was born for you, dear. We were not born for each other, after all — were we, dear? I am the woman of that poem, not Isabel. It is I who must say good-bye. I can do it. I am a woman now, love — not a little child any more. 'Look in my face and see.'"

The tangle of Theophil's emotions and thoughts, as he listened to Jenny in silence, was a revelation to him of the strange heart of love, and of the insufficiency of those formulas by which we image ourselves to ourselves. How little we know of ourselves till we are tested by the powerful reagents of love and danger, and in how many ways must those tests be applied before we learn anything of the elements of which we are composed!

One love will reveal to us one side of our natures and its needs, another will reveal to us another with its needs; and till we grow old we can never be certain that there are not other sides to us that have never been illuminated, other needs that have never been awakened, by an emotion.

A man may love two women equally: the woman he most needs and the woman who needs him most, — and in a crisis of choice he will probably choose the latter.

Again, the power of the woman we have loved first has wonderful reserves to draw upon, humble pawns of feelings, memories, associations, not so brilliant to the imagination as the royalties of romance and sentiment on the other side, but incalculably useful in a battle. Too humble are some of these to gain acknowledgment; indeed they are often so submerged in a total of vague impulses that they escape any individualisation.

In the very hour where all seemed lost to Jenny, Theophil's love for her was passing in the fire of this ordeal from a love whose elements had never, perhaps, quite combined, into that miraculous metal of true love, which can never again be separated into anything but itself, — the true gold of love which, in some magical second of projection, has suddenly sprung out of those troubled ingredients of earth and iron, silver, honey, and pearl.

This does not mean that Theophil's love for Isabel had grown any less real, but that his love for Jenny had grown more real. For the first time in its history it moved on the stage of the heroic. Up till now it had lived secure, domestic days; there had been no danger to test its truth, no lights of tragedy or romance thrown across it, it had seemed a simple little earthborn love; whereas Theophil's love for Isabel had, from its very conditions, walked from the first the high heaven of dreams.

Isabel, indeed, still remained the heavenly love, but those who understand will know the strength of Jenny when I say that she became confirmed in this hour of trial as the household love of Theophil's life. Isabel remained the Muse, but it was Jenny, after all, in spite of those solemn words in the Wood of Silence, that was the wife; and if, at first sound, there seems less of heaven in such a love, it is surely only because when heaven has become incarnated upon earth we forget to call it heaven.

In the few moments of silence which followed Jenny's words, it was some such turmoil of feelings and thoughts, questionings and conclusions, which passed through Theophil's mind, at last resolving itself into words that sounded unexpected even in his own ears.

"Jenny," he said, "it is quite true that I love Isabel and that she loves me. But it is true that I love you too, love you more truly in this moment than I have ever loved you, and that no other woman can ever take your place. If you give me up for Isabel's sake, it will be no gain to her, for I would not go to her. I love you, indeed I love you, and I want no other woman to be my wife."

Jenny's face brightened for a moment;

they were good words, and they sounded real. But then that embrace, how real that was; nothing again could ever be so real as that!

"Ah, Theophil dear; but you stood as though you loved her so; your arms were so tender, it was just as though they said 'wife.' You are deceiving yourself, dear, believe me, you are. God knows how I love you; I have nothing in the world but you, and if . . . if . . ."

"Jenny, try and believe; let me show you how I can love you. I seem never to have shown you before. Let us begin our love over again from to-night. I know your heart is bleeding, but let me heal it, dear. I know this sorrow must lie heavy upon us for a long while yet, but it will pass, you shall see. O you shall see how I love you. Let us be married soon, dear; let us wait no longer . . ."

Theophil had raised his head, and as he spoke poured on Jenny all the appeal of his strong eyes; with all the might of his soul he willed her back to happiness, as Orpheus strove by his singing to bring back Eurydice from the shades. She could not look into his set longing face without feeling that he was speaking true words. Hope flickered for a moment in her sad eyes; yes! he wanted to come back to her; he wanted to be hers again.

But was it not too late? Hadn't something gone forever, something been killed? Could even Theophil himself ever make her happy any more? Then the misery flooded over her again in an irresistible sea, in which all kind words fell powerless as snowflakes; her resolution broke down, and with terrible sobs she flung herself into Theophil's arms.

"O Theophil, my heart is breaking, my heart is breaking."

Theophil was to feel her crying thus against his bosom till the end of his life. He shuddered with dread at this terrible crying — it was as though all her life was leaving her in sobs, as though she were bleeding to death in tears. It was grief piteously prostrate, wild, convulsive, unutterable. Jenny was right. Her heart was breaking. Theophil's terror was right. It was too late to love her. This was the death-crying of a broken heart.

CHAPTER XXI

IN WHICH JENNY IS MYSTERIOUSLY HONOURED

STILL a moment did at last come when the sobs subsided, and Jenny dried her tears. She was going to try, try to be happy again, try to forget it; and she tried so well that in a few days her face had grown even bright again, — bright as silver. It could never again be bright as gold.

And Theophil's love was like a sun pouring down upon her day by day. Yes, he loved her. She could not doubt that, though there were times when his true words and caresses suddenly seemed to wear a torturing falsity, as she thought of Isabel.

But such feelings she put from her bravely. Jealous of Isabel in the common way she had not been. She herself loved her too well, and soon she was able to talk of her again to Theophil. They had agreed that Isabel should not know what Jenny had seen that night of the recital. For Jenny could not bear to think of the letters it would mean. "Let that be our secret, dear," she said to Theophil; and thus, when Isabel wrote, she wrote back in her usual way. Theophil and Isabel never wrote to each other. It was no part of their love to deceive Jenny in letters. Their love was vowed to silence and absence, and in Theophil's life it must be more and more of a starlit background.

So the weeks went by, and the marriage of Theophil and Jenny was now finally fixed for the 12th of February. On second thoughts, as their love grew serene once more, they had decided not to anticipate that date, for old Mrs. Talbot's sake; and meanwhile Jenny was admonished by that old mother to make haste and get that flesh on her bones.

ZION CHAPEL

The admonition was not without cause, for it presently became noticeable that Jenny was not merely negatively disobeying her old mother in this. Not only was she not growing fatter, but, indeed, she was, for one reason or another, slowly and almost imperceptibly growing thinner. It was not those at home who noticed this first, but outside friends, who, suddenly meeting her, would remark that she wasn't looking half the girl she used to be.

She had already begun to remark it herself, as with her bare arms she would coil up her hair, standing before her mirror; and she thought nothing of it till one day, as she stood there, she noticed a curious expression flash into her face and go again almost before she could mark it. Her face, which had always been round and plump, seemed suddenly to gaze back at her, very narrow and pinched and white, strangely sunken, too, and rigid. It was all a mere flash and gone again, and her real face was presently back once more.

But the look filled her with solemn thoughts, in which she was surprised to find a certain comfort, as of a sad wish fulfilling itself.

She spoke to no one of that look, but it must have been the same look that Theophil saw, a few nights after, as she sat listening to him reading in her usual chair. Suddenly, as he looked up at her, he threw down the book, and with concern, almost terror, in his voice, exclaimed, "Good God, Jenny! are you ill, dear? What is that terrible white look in your face?"

He sprang across and took her hands. The look had gone again before he had finished speaking, but it was a look he was never to forget.

One day Jenny put out her arm, and asked him to feel how thin it was growing.

"It *is* thin, dear; but you mustn't be anxious. Perhaps you're a trifle run down. You must see the doctor."

ZION CHAPEL 177

Mrs. Talbot did not believe in doctors, and suggested nourishing soups and port wine as a substitute. These, however, made those dear arms no fatter, they put none of that promised flesh on Jenny's bones. (Why did Theophil rather creep one day as Mrs. Talbot made use of that expression?)

And Jenny was growing tired too. She was not so ready on her feet as she used to be. Small exertions exhausted her. Her breath was not so available for running up and down stairs as it had been.

Then Theophil would have a doctor, who sounded Jenny, and looked a little grave, but finally, reassured, asked her if she had had a shock, — Jenny smiled rather knowingly, but denied it, — declared her a little run down and in need of bracing and nourishment, prescribed phosphites and steel.

Then Jenny got very wet one day on her way from school, and she began to cough. She had to stay at home, and bed was perhaps the best place for her. So Jenny went to bed, and looked very pretty there, and was quite merry of an evening when Theophil, bringing her flowers, — he was already bringing her flowers, — would draw up the arm-chair by her side, and read to her. Those were very sweet hours, perhaps the sweetest their love had ever known, so cosy and homelike, and yet without fear.

But one evening, when Jenny had been coughing, there was blood on the bosom of her nightdress, and as Theophil saw it, his heart stood still with terror. Jenny grew very white, too, as she saw it, though the awful thought which was behind the still look they gave each other was not quite new to her. Sometimes she might have been heard softly saying over to herself, —

"I am lost, I am changed, I must go farther, where
The change shall take me worse, and no one dare
Look in my face and see."

Yet although Death's voice calling us from afar may seem all sweetness, his voice coming nearer has a note of dread in it that appals the most death-desirous heart. And in that silence those poor lovers both heard him singing, it seemed not many streets away.

"I must be very ill, dear," said Jenny. "O my love, O my love . . . !"

Theophil strove with himself to say words with a real ring of the future in them, when this cloud should have passed away; and for his sake Jenny pretended to believe them. Yes, this very week he would take her away to bright skies and healing air, — though Jenny felt a little tired at the thought of rising any more from the bed to which she was growing curiously accustomed.

Then there came a new doctor to see Jenny. He was a very clever specialist from a distant town; but for him the business of death had not yet obscured its tragedy, — though words like "tragedy" were not often on his tongue. Consumption was a strong enough word for him.

His heart went out to that little household; and when he saw Jenny, it ached for that young man downstairs. It was more than a professional contempt for the "general practitioner" that made him silently curse what he called the "death-doctor," as he looked at Jenny, "Jack of all diseases, and master of none."

"Two months ago, a month," he thought, as he listened and listened for a sound of hope that might come to his ear through Jenny's wasted side, — "even a month, and I could have saved her." And yet as he talked to her he was not so sure, after all. He missed something in her voice. It was the will to live.

"Have you had a shock at any time?" he said.

Jenny was taken by surprise for a moment, — the other doctor had asked her that, too, — and she did not deny it so convincingly as she tried to.

"O, that's all right," said the doctor aloud to Jenny and her mother, who stood by, though inwardly he said, "I see. That's the reason;" and again he said, "I'm afraid you mustn't get up just yet. That chest of yours has to be taken care of, but you needn't be anxious. In a month or six weeks you'll be all right again."

"Only a month or six weeks," said Jenny, with a sinking voice. She meant — was that all that was left to her of life and love?

Downstairs Theophil stood waiting with a beating heart. He sprang to the door and drew the doctor into his room. The doctor laid a kind hand upon his arm, and there was a look in his face that made Theophil's heart die within him.

"You mean she is going to die?" he said with fearful calmness. "*You mean that?*"

"My poor fellow, God knows what I would give to deny it."

"She — is — going — to — die — *to die!* It is impossible! Not Jenny!" and between that exclamation and his first stunned cry it seemed as though bells had been tolling a thousand years. It seemed as though he had been sitting there as in a cave since the beginning of time, saying over and over to himself, "Jenny is going to die."

There was a decanter on the sideboard. The doctor poured some spirit into a glass. "Drink this," he said. Theophil drank it raw, as though it had been water; and presently a certain illusive hope began to stir like an opening rose in his brain, and when the doctor had gone he turned to that decanter again. Perhaps if he drank enough he would find that Jenny was not to die, after all. At all events, the spirit gave him nerve, which else he could not have found, to go and sit by Jenny once more. It helped him even to be gay, so that Jenny said to herself, "The doctor has not told him that I am going to die."

"The doctor said I shall be better in

a month or six weeks," she said aloud, and tried to look as though she were happy.

"Didn't I say so, dearie?" said old Mrs. Talbot, whom, curiously, love made blind instead of prophet-sighted.

"Yes; and then we'll go together to those blue skies and that bright air," said Theophil.

"Yes, dear," said Jenny, closing her eyes wearily.

Presently she opened them again, and said, "Won't you read something to me, Theophil?"

"What shall I read, dear?"

"Something amusing, love. 'Alice in the Looking-Glass,' eh? It's such a long time since we read that. Don't you remember how once long ago we could never get the Walrus and the Carpenter out of our heads?"

So Theophil read the hallowed nonsense once again, struck with the fantastic incongruity of the moment. Even the dying have to go on living, and must be treated like living folks, — for a little while longer; and, though they are slipping away, slipping away, under your very eyes, there are merciful hours when you forget that they are dying. You read to them, talk to them, gossip about neighbours, — they are going to die, and yet they are quite interested in Mrs. Smith's new baby, — you laugh together over little jokes in the newspapers, and then suddenly the bell of your thoughts goes tolling: "They are going to die — have you forgotten they are going to die? — Think! there is so much to say before they go — O, think of it all — miss nothing, watch their faces every moment of the day — for soon you shall torture yourself in vain to remember just that curve of the mouth, that droop of the chin. Ask them everything now — tell them all — delay not — take farewell of that voice, that laugh, those living eyes — for they — are going to die."

Death was kind as long as he might be to Jenny's face, so that for some days old Mrs. Talbot still failed to see his shadowy mark there; but at last she knew what Jenny and Theophil had both striven to hide from her and from each other.

"My poor little girl, my poor boy!" she said over and over to herself from that time, but she did not cry or break down.

It was a pathetic sign of what was coming, that she now allowed Theophil sometimes to be Jenny's nurse through the night hours. There was to be no bridal bed for these lovers, but thus the tender quiet hours of the night were theirs even in so sad a fashion.

One night, in the haunted hushed middle of it, the old mother had softly pushed open the door to ask if all went well, and in a whisper Theophil had assured her. A night-light gave an uncanny shadow-breeding light in the room. Jenny was sleeping peacefully, her tired ivory face, with her dark elf-locks falling about it, framed on the pillow. Theophil raised himself softly in his chair and looked at her. She would sleep some while yet. Then from sheer weariness — grief's best friend — he too fell into a light sleep. From this he was awakened with a start. Jenny was sitting up and bending over him. With her dark hair hanging about her face, and in that light, there was something weird and unearthly about her, as though she were already dead and had risen in her shroud. Something of a shiver went through him, as she put her thin arms round his neck and clutched him in a sudden agony of longing. All the strength of her poor little body seemed to pass into that kiss, so eager, so convulsive. "Jenny dear, it will make you so ill; lie down, little girl" — and Jenny fell back on her pillow exhausted and coughing, and with eyes unearthly bright.

"Theophil," she said suddenly, in that startling way sick people have, "you know that I am going to die!"

He could not answer, his voice would have choked in sobs. He leaned his head close to Jenny and pressed her hand, and in spite of himself two great tears fell upon Jenny's cheek.

But Jenny was curiously calm. There was almost a note of scolding in her voice, as she said, "It's no use crying, Theophil — it's got to be borne."

She was already growing strangely wise, and a little removed from earth. The first fears of her dark journey were passing, as she was more and more sinking among the shadows. In moments there seemed to be something almost trivial in earthly grief. But there was still one earthly joy, one earthly pride, of which her soul began to conceive the desire. It had come with the thought of her grave that one day took her, less with fear, than of a new home to which she would presently be going. In her fancy she had seen her name: "*Jenny Talbot, the beloved daughter of John and Jane Talbot, aged twenty-one years,"* and it had struck her that the name was wrong.

Talbot? that was not her name. This was not the legend of her days. The world would be all wrong about her if it only read that in after days. No, her tomb could only bear one inscription — and what sweetness amid all the bitterness of death there was to say it over and over again to herself: *"Jenny Londonderry, the beloved wife of Theophilus Londonderry, aged twenty-one years."*

Only twenty-one years — she thought of those who would perhaps some day stand and read those words and think "What a sad little life!" — and yet all that mattered of life had been lived in those short years, aye, in two of them, and the violet breath of young love would come up to those who read from her young grave, as it would never breathe from the earth of long-wed, late-dying lovers.

Perhaps it was a beautiful chance for love to end like theirs; their love had never grown old, so it would remain forever young, a spring sign, a star in the front of love's year for ever.

Jenny spoke her wish to Theophil in the quiet of that night. The wish had been in his heart too, and the wish was presently fulfilled. Brides have seldom been happier than Jenny as she looked on the wife's ring that hung loose on her thin finger, and brides have often been sadder.

Death was coming very near now, so near that Jenny began to forget that she was going to die. She forgot too that she was married to Theophil, and would sometimes babble her heart-breaking fancies of the little home that was so near now, till sometimes Theophil had to hurry away with his unbearable grief to some other room.

And Jenny's once rosy apple of a face made one's heart ache to look on now. It made one frightened, too: it was so dark and witchlike, so uncanny, almost

wicked, so thin and full of inky shadows.
She would sit up in her bed a wizened
little goblin, and laugh a queer, dry,
knowing laugh to herself, — a laugh like
the scraping of reeds in a solitary place.
A strange black weariness seemed to be
crushing down her brows, like the "un-
willing sleep" of a strong narcotic. She
would begin a sentence and let it wither
away unfinished, and point sadly and
almost humorously to her straight black
hair, clammy as the feathers of a dead
bird lying in the rain. Her hearing was
strangely keen. And yet she did not
know, was not to know. How was one
to talk to her — talk of being well again,
and books and country walks, when she
had so plainly done with all these things?
How bear it, when she, with a half-sad,
half-amused smile, showed her thin wrists?
How say that they would soon be strong
and round again? Ugh! she was already
beginning to be different from us, already
putting off our body-sweet mortality, and

putting on the fearful garments of death, changing from ruddy familiar humanity into a being of another element, — an element we dread as the fish dreads the air. Soon we should not be able to talk to her. Soon she would have unlearnt all the sweet grammar of earth. She was no longer Jenny, but a fearful symbol of mysteries at which the flesh crept. She was going to die.

It was a bitterly cold night toward the end of January when Jenny died. She had been curiously alert and restless all the afternoon. Once when Theophil and she had been alone, she beckoned him with a grave, significant gesture to her side. She was lying down, and she made as if she would sit up. Humouring her, Theophil raised her and packed up the pillows at her back. Then, with indescribable solemnity, she took his face in her hands and kissed him. "Do you love me, Theophil?" she said. "Will you ever forget me?"

"I will love you for ever. I will never forget you."

He took her gently in his arms, and with terrible tenderness she held him close to her for a moment, and then sank back with a sigh. For a moment he thought she was dead; but presently she revived, though that was the last flicker of Jenny's conscious life.

Towards evening she began to take strange fancies, which had to be humoured. She complained of intruding faces in the room, she called with dreadful peevishness to unseen people who would not leave her bedside, and even sat at its foot. Then she forgot them, and imagined she was picking daisies on the counterpane. Then she begged Theophil to go downstairs and see Isabel. It was a shame to keep her waiting all that time by herself in the study. And when Theophil tried to persuade her that Isabel was not there, she shook her head and said: "You must not mind me, Theophil, dear. I'm not un-

ZION CHAPEL

happy about her now. I'm not a silly little girl any more. I'm a woman now. 'Look in my face and see.'"

Then towards midnight a sudden accession of strength came to her, and she said she would get up. They tried to dissuade her; she grew angry, and struggled so hard to rise, that it seemed best to humour her once more. So, wrapt round with blankets, Theophil lifted her from the bed into a great chair by the fire. Then she asked to be taken to look into her bottom drawer. So they lifted her across to it, and opened it. She dabbled with her hands aimlessly among its piteous treasures, laughing low to herself.

Suddenly a fit of coughing took her, and a great choking was in her throat. She was seen to be battling for her breath. For an instant she drew herself up, and lifted her hand as though she would wave farewell, smiled a faint little smile at Theophil, making, too, as if she would speak. Then she fell back, her whole body relaxed, she had ceased coughing, and a wonderful sweetness was stealing over her face. She had gone all alone into the darkness, and Theophil was alone in the world.

ZION CHAPEL 195

CHAPTER XXII

THE TRYST LETHEAN

JENNY had gone into the darkness, and she had gone alone. Theophil had not gone with her.

That he had remained behind meant certainly no selfish clinging to life, and indeed there was a sense, as was presently to appear, in which very really he had kept young love's old promise and died with Jenny. That he had not literally fulfilled it was due to those physical conditions of dying of which in the hour of that promise young love is happily ignorant; for the promise is usually made in moments of keenly conscious physical life. Dying together is then figured, perhaps, as climbing hand in hand the radiant topmost peak of life, with a last splendid leap together into some immortal morning; and such a marriage in death, a last union of two lives in some fiery consummation of dying, has been the lot of some lovers supremely blest.

Some indeed there are whose last earthly moment is a vivid reassertion of the glory and loveliness of life. They drink the great cup to its last golden drain, and by their death-beds we seem to be standing at the laughing founts of being. They are radiant, victorious, even witty, to the last, when at one swoop of blackness they are extinguished like a light plunged into a stream.

But for others the cold mists that hang low by Lethe's banks have already brought forgetfulness before their feet grow icy with the first step into the dark water. To meet on Lethe-side is to meet, maybe; but with a sad unrecognising meeting. To lie together in oblivion, with sightless eyes, and dulled hearts and listless hands,—that was not love's meaning.

ZION CHAPEL

And not only are the dying thus drugged out of knowledge before they die, but those who stand near them grow drowsed, too, by the fumes of the poppies of death. The dying have forgotten; the living are numb and foolish and in a dream. All they love on earth is passing away beneath their very eyes, and they cannot understand,—cannot realise that this, *this* is death.

Except in moments of piercing agony, days and weeks afterwards, moments that were similarly soothed away again by that mysterious narcotic property which pain at its highest brings with it (pain at its highest being its own anæsthetic), Theophil never realised that Jenny had died, and least of all at the moment when she was dying. Long after he remembered how he had said to himself: "There is Jenny dying, dying. A few more seconds and she will be beyond the sound of your voice for ever. Call to her; she can still, perhaps, hear you. O my

Jenny, my Jenny! Louder, louder,—hold her tighter, tighter,—she is slipping away. O God, she is slipping away. No love can hold her back. My Jenny, my Jenny!"

And all the time he had been curiously calm, almost unfeeling,—as one standing stupefied in the presence of fate. The air seemed full of boding sounds, echoes of low thunder, as from a distant world in the throes of portentous change; and he told himself mechanically that he should know the meaning of those sounds some day. He should wake up soon from this unnatural torpor of pain to an empty house of life, through the cold halls of which he would seek in vain for Jenny for evermore.

Meanwhile, he suddenly found himself standing with his back to the fire in the lighted study, talking to Mr. Moggridge, who, late as was the hour, had called for news, and had stayed on from a perception that the young minister had best have some one to talk to as far into the morning as he would go on talking. They were talking in a business-like way of Zion; and Theophil was smoking cigarette after cigarette. He was terribly clear-headed and bright-witted, and Mr. Moggridge looked at him sometimes with a sort of fear.

It was about three in the morning when the door was softly opened by Mrs. Talbot.

"Will you come now, and see our little girl?" she said, with a voice that could say no more.

Theophil followed her, and, still in a dream, he stood in Jenny's room, grown strangely solemn and sweet since he was last there, — was it a thousand years ago? And there was Jenny lying asleep with a wonderful smile on her face. She had a little gold chain round her neck and a white crysanthemum in the bosom of her night-gown, and you thought of some princess lying in enchanted sleep in an Arabian night. It seemed so light a sleep and yet somehow so eternal. You stept softly, you spoke low, lest you should awaken her — not carelessly shall one disturb that imperious slumber.

Yes, the distinction of death sat like an invisible crown upon Jenny's brow. She was no longer little Jenny, but a mysterious princess upon whose sleep it was permitted thus to gaze. The pain which had filled these weeks with bitter human anguish had been the process of some mysterious ennoblement. She had been found "worthy to die." In the peerage of God's creatures, she had now outsoared those whom she loved. The nature of it was a mystery, but no one could look on her face and doubt that a great honour had come to little Jenny.

But, O Jenny, may it be your gain indeed, for the loss to us is greater than we can bear — greater than we can bear. Not Theophil only — not young love, that, for all his smitten heart, has somewhere hidden away the potencies of his unspent life, and will still have his dream, though sorrow itself should become that dream — but this poor old mother, all the force of her days spent, the sap of her spirit dried up. Hers is the terrible sorrow of age, with not a hope left betwixt her and death.

Pity her, Jenny — speak one word to her. Hearken to her sobs as she kneels by your side, and can you not hear the hard crying of his heart that knows no tears?

Are you become as the gods, Jenny, that you still smile on at the sound of mortal tears? Will you not stretch out one of those folded hands to each and lead them away with you? They are praying to follow you, only to be with you, wherever you are.

And it did seem as though in some strange way the soul of the mother had still some sure communication with the soul of her dead child. Motherhood had given her a nearness in the hour which no love of a lover could gain. She alone spoke to the dead girl as though she were still really alive, as one speaking to the deaf whom only one voice can reach.

But Theophil was conscious in his wildest, most heartbroken, words that Jenny could not hear them. He talked to her as though she were a picture of herself, and as one would implore a picture to answer us, he symbolised the cry of his soul in cries that he knew were vain.

Yet though Jenny were sculpture now, Theophil could not forget that this icy marble had once been the flesh he had loved. O God! that little tender body, whose every part was sweetly joined together like the words of a song, it was marble now.

"Ah! Jenny, are you smiling to think of what you and I know, you and I, and no one else in the world? Jenny, we shall never forget, never forget, shall we? And you will not breathe our secrets even in heaven. Do you really hear me, after all, but are forbidden to say? Are you glad somewhere to see how I love you, and are you at this moment looking into my face wildly for a sign, as I into yours? Is it I who seem dead, Jenny? and are you beating wildly at the gates of life to win back to me, as I am beating at the gates of death? But, Jenny, we shall find each other, *must* find each other some day. I shall be so true, Jenny, — will you be true to me in heaven?"

Then would sweep across his soul a pitiless vista of the long cold years that lay between him and Jenny. He was not twenty-five; through what a weary pilgrimage of useless years must he journey on, before there was Jenny's face shining at the end. How he envied the old woman whose sorrow was in this alone less cruel than his, that she was already fifty years farther on the road to Jenny. Perhaps another year or two and she would meet her. To meet so soon — was hardly to have parted at all.

But, why live those years? Have you forgotten that old promise? Is it too late to follow? Surely little Jenny will not speed so swiftly from the earth she loved but that you shall overtake her. Who knows but she is fluttering still at the gate of death, putting off the heavenward journey hour after hour, in hope that the face she waits for will at last light up the dark portal —

> " I 'll take his hand and go with him
> To the deep wells of light ;
> As unto a stream we will step down,
> And bathe there in God's sight."

But was this the way to find Jenny? The universe was so full of dark traps for lovers' feet. To lie down cold as Jenny by Jenny's side, was that the way to find her? When death's gate opened for Jenny, had Theophil at that very instant, hand in her hand, eyes fixed upon her eyes, slipped through too, then surely they had been together. But the door had closed, and whither on the other side Jenny had already wandered, who could tell? Perhaps that was the very way to miss her.

When two have lost each other in a crowd, it is best that one should stand still and await the other. Perhaps it were best for him to stand still here in life. Jenny would know where to seek him then — and maybe the dead had mysterious ways of bringing news to the living. He could wait a little while and see. For a little he could live — and listen.

CHAPTER XXIII

JENNY'S LYING IN STATE

BUT there were others besides those who stood so near who mourned Jenny, passers-by on the road of friendship, who would miss her sunshine in the streets, and carry with them one bright thought the less for that bright face that death had thus blown out. There were especially some little people to whom death was as yet hardly even mysterious, but was merely perplexing, like many other grown-up things in which their parents were interested. These were the little scholars of Jenny's Sunday-school class, to whom simple Jenny had been a personage, quite a great lady, full of gentleness. To these Jenny was "Teacher," a name of gentle awe; and

ZION CHAPEL

to these Teacher was as deeply dear as anyone can be to very young hearts.

Jenny had felt like a little mother to these little ones, and when she lay ill her thoughts would often go to them, while from them would come tiny presents to show how sorry they were that Teacher was ill.

Several times before she grew too ill, Jenny had had her favourites up in her room on Sunday evenings, to read Bible stories with her, and had sent them away happy with magnificent text-cards, that had hitherto been the arduously won rewards of "attention" and the practice of such school-time virtues over many weeks.

Now, when they heard that Teacher was dead, they felt a vague sorrow. They knew that people who died were never seen at school any more, and that people always burst out crying when anyone died; so they cried bitterly, these little girls, and the hearts of one or two of them perhaps really ached for a little while. One of them asked the new teacher, if they would meet their old teacher in heaven, and was told "Yes, if they were good girls," — which was something to be good for.

Among the wreaths that already filled Jenny's room with that piercing smell of lilies which still clung there — unless it were Theophil's fancy — for many months afterwards, was one sent in loving memory "by her Sunday-school class"; and it was a part of that informal lying-in-state, which is an involuntary recognition of the divine honours due to death, that these little awestruck scholars should be taken in threes and fours to look at Teacher for the last time.

·This was the third day, and Jenny was already in her coffin. The first bloom of death, that light that lingers awhile in the face like a sunset tranquil and blessed, a smile of immortal promise in the very moment of mortality, had faded. Jenny's face by this was really dead, a mask of drawn and sunken wax. She seemed now

ZION CHAPEL

some fantastic doll, some ghastly waxwork image of death such as we see carried on the stage in tragic plays. The reality of death had gone with the coming of its funereal trappings. But the little girls, who had to be lifted up one by one to gaze with curious, scared faces into that harsh box, deeper and deeper into which, as through beds of flowers and veils of gauze, Teacher was sinking, knew nothing of these thoughts. They looked and wondered in hushed bewilderment, and went their ways. It was evidently an occasion when children were to keep more than usually quiet — and was it really Teacher in that strange deep box? It was rather meaningless, but it was certainly very strange and solemn, and you were allowed to cry.

Of the others who came to see Jenny, I shall not speak, — the vulgar sight-seers, the creepy old women, connoisseurs in beautiful death, for whom a neighbour's funeral was like an invitation to the grand opera, but on whom perhaps one should not be too severe, for even such coarse sensitiveness to a mystery is the crude beginning of the poetic.

The night before Jenny was given back to the elements Theophil dreamed a dream, and afterwards he liked to think that he had dreamed it while Jenny's body was still in the house with him, for then it might be interpreted that her spirit was still there too, waiting for its final release from the clay which God had sent her to animate for a while, as an artist imprisons a lovely thought in a vase of alabaster.

Theophil dreamed that he and some friends were gay together in a room, just before setting out for a theatre; and as they laughed and talked there came a little tapping on the wall, so that they grew silent and listened. Then through the wall was heard a faint but glad little voice speaking. It was Jenny's voice.

"I can hear you all," she said; "you are off to the theatre. I wish I were going with you. Never mind, we are not so far away from each other as you think. I am only on the other side of a wall."

And Theophil awoke on a bright wintry morning, with those words still, it seemed, in the room.

"I am only on the other side of a wall!" Was it but the metaphor-making of dreams, which will so often take our forgotten speculations and dramatise them for us into reality, or was it indeed a message? An instinct which was unamenable to reason, and which was perhaps only a desire, told him it was a message; and it was no less a message though it were merely a pictorial symbol of a sense, which was already his in the daytime, of a new and very real nearness to Jenny.

He had slept right through that night out of sheer bodily weariness. Weeks of watching and anguish had worn him out, and he never knew that the poor old mother had laid a benediction on his sleep, looking in upon him as he slept, the only waking being in that house of sleep.

"He will wake soon enough, poor boy!" she had said, as she went once more to watch till daylight by the side of the other sleeper.

"O Jenny, Jenny, why did you leave me? You were the apple of my eye, my Jenny. What will your old mother do now that you are gone?"

So she sat and wailed hour after hour, and sometimes she would raise the dead girl from her coffin and press her to her bosom; for, though even Jenny's lover feared her now, that cold unresponsive clay had no fear for Jenny's mother. It was Jenny still, and though the old woman's creed told her that Jenny was already an angel in heaven, her heart belied her faith, and her love made her a Sadducee.

And yet it was her belief in a literal resurrection of the body that was sorely troubling her old soul during these last hours of watching. For while Jenny was still conscious of the coming of death, she had been much tortured by hideous churchyard fancies, imaginations of the darkness and noisomeness of the grave, and she had wrung from her mother the promise that she should first be cremated and her ashes be afterward buried in the family tomb. This was the promise which was lying heavy on the old woman's heart to-night; and, though her reason told her that the way of the flames and the way of the flowers alike led to dust, yet the disintegration by fire seemed to give her a sense of entire destruction such as the more desultory operations of the earth did not give.

If Jenny must indeed pass right away, the dainty architecture of her body, so lovingly builded, be laid in ruin; not by the fierce fingers of fire should she be torn asunder, but beneath the kind breath of the sun, and the gentle tears of the rain, might she change and change, and on the wings of soft winds might she be carried to and fro in fragrance about the world.

And perhaps in the old Christian's mind there was an imagination of a mysterious recreation in the earth, which when the dust has quite returned to dust, should begin anew the building of an incorruptible Jenny, lying prepared there like a new garment, against the hour when the soul should seek anew its earthly vesture for the last great day. Thus strangely will imagination build its dreams in defiance of imagination.

And in what different ways will love argue with itself! This way of the flames, that brought such a terror to the poor mother, was one of the great consolations of the lover; and when at length on the morrow Jenny was no longer to be sought in her room, and the darkened house was once more filled with an empty light that was crueller than darkness, it brought a sense of warmth to think that Jenny was not lying stark and lonely out in that bitter churchyard, where the graves were covered with sheets of snow and hung with hoods of ice, but that through the cleansing gates of flame she had passed into the eternal elements, and was already about the business of the dreaming spring.

And in other ways this proved a consolation that never failed him. It saved his love from those cruel foulnesses of the grave which had haunted Jenny. That cleansing fire cleansed his fancies too. However morbid his fancies might become, *desiderium* could never take any but beautiful forms. Jenny could never come to him in any fearful images of corruption, nor could he picture her in any mouldering shape of catacomb or charnel.

She had come like a sylph out of the air, and she had returned again whence she came. She had moved awhile about certain ever sacred rooms, and as she moved she had hummed a little song, which was her life; she had touched certain objects, she had written her name in some books, she had made little everlasting memories with her hands, — that was her history; and now suddenly she had gone. She had come like a dream, and she had gone like a dream. The invisible winds had for a while rocked a flower, and now the flower was gone. Only its perfume remained. No one as long as the world lasted could take up some crumbling relic, and, giving the lie to love's divine answer to the dust, say " This was Jenny ! "

No! but sometimes when a bird sings in the stillness, when the moon rises above the trees, when a breath of secret violets crosses one's path one knows not whence; sometimes when the rain is sobbing at the window, or the wind plaining about the doors; sometimes when an unknown happiness fills the heart, when a great deed has been done, when a lovely word has been spoken, in seasons of music and in all high moments, then can one say, " There, listen! *that* was Jenny."

Jenny was already a legend. She was

with the great lovers. Theophil remained behind only to write her name across the high stars. Then he, too, would pass through the gates of fire to her side.

As he lay down to rest that night, his eyes fell with a sudden sense of freshness upon the familiar Botticelli's "Mother and Child," which hung over his fireplace; and a need that could never be fulfilled awoke in his soul. If only Jenny could have left him a little child,—a little girl! He had not seemed so lonely then.

It was so he thought; yet perhaps Jenny's child would but have deepened his loneliness, like a bird singing in a garden where our love walked long ago. Yet the cry was from his heart, and the longing brought with it his first tears. "O Jenny," he sobbed, "if only you had left me a little child!"

CHAPTER XXIV

THE BEGINNING OF THE PILGRIMAGE — A MESSAGE FROM JENNY

IF every inclination of his heart had not desired it too, Theophil would have gone on living at 3 Zion Place, for old Mrs. Talbot's sake; for now he was literally all she had left in the world, and what greater joy remained for either than just to sit close by the fire and talk of Jenny?

3 Zion Place was now a little chapel of memory, where a bowed ancient woman and a sad-faced young man kept up perpetual services to the holy dead. A woman of her own years, also acquainted with grief, came to companion the old woman, a sort of lay sister in this little monastery of grief.

It was so piety began, and thus piety is purest and tenderest in the worship of the dead. Everything in that house which had taken the impress of Jenny's fingers, been Jenny's to use or handle, remained exactly as and where Jenny had placed it. They were as yet as fragrant of Jenny as a fresh-gathered flower of its own perfume. In a very real sense indeed Jenny had not died, or she was coming to life again as she had never lived before; and it was no merely idealised Jenny who was henceforward to fill up all her lover's thoughts and speak to him in every sight and sound, but just the human Jenny, with her faults and all.

On these — such little faults ! — Theophil ever loved to dwell. They saved Jenny from becoming an abstraction, a saint. Even those bitter little quarrels which all lovers must suffer, — how sweet they seemed now!

The old mother's method was no doubt again different from her son-in-law's. She would never have admitted that Jenny had a fault. Such is the difference in reality between the new idealism and the old.

In such small matters as the minutiæ of mourning that difference was again illustrated. Theophil could permit himself no outward insignia of sorrow which he could not wear for ever. Already his profession had clothed him in black, and it was only for him that his black seemed now to gain a deeper distinction; but such ugly symbols of beautiful memory as that notepaper whose diminishing edge of blackness is rather a cynical witness of a graduated forgetfulness, were not for a real grief like his. As if sorrow, while it may and will change, can ever end! Why, in the world of faithful hearts, men and women have not yet dried their tears for Romeo and Juliet!

Theophil conceived this grief that had come to him as one more activity added to his life till life should end. He knew that it would not outcast joy, but that it would live side by side with it, that it

ZION CHAPEL

must alternate with joy for it to go on living. Jenny's death was not going to be less sad, less a factor of the eternal tragedy, at the end of a year,— that he might go to a theatre once more, as some widows joyously don colours, when the clock strikes the end of a year of lost dances.

For it was not Jenny alone that had died, but it was a consolation to Theophil in those hours of self-torture which are among the earliest and most cruel developments of grief, to realise how much of himself had died with her, after all. It was not merely the apathy of the first weeks that told him this, the sense of vacuity, of uselessness in all things, but the sense that never left him, even when he had awakened to an activity he had never known before, that nothing really mattered, however vigorously he might seem to act to the contrary, since Jenny had gone.

It was with difficulty sometimes that he could take important issues with necessary seriousness, for, whatever the odds of life henceforward might be, what was there worth gaining now that Jenny was lost? Could any energy or haste save Jenny from dying? That had happened. The worst had happened. All the terror life had to appal the human spirit had been faced, in that moment when the doctor's hand upon his shoulder had told him Jenny was to die. His eyes had looked on the Medusa-face of life that turns the bravest to stone, and he was no longer vulnerable humanity.

On the battle-field of existence he bore a charmed life, and sometimes as he moved among his fellows he felt a certain sense of the unfairness of his advantage in this respect, and paused to pity those who could still be so eager, so tragically set upon, this little issue. The virulence of those enemies whom he was already making and who were to multiply as his activities awakened again, seemed particularly pathetic, and he would smile in sad amusement at their quaint little efforts to hurt him. (No man is so strong for this world's fight as he who has laid up his treasure in heaven; and when the mystic condescends to the common trades of life he is an easy master.) It meant so much to them, so little to him. He was a humbug, he was a hypocrite, he wasn't even a good speaker, he was an ignoramus! Was he? All right. They might think so if they chose. It hardly interested him. He had been sitting drawing angels, and somehow their irrelevant voices had broken in upon him. "Another was with me."

Really, even for Jenny's sake, it seemed hardly worth while to fight so poor a world! Was the fame that such a world could give a distinction one would seek for Jenny? Would not Jenny smile in heaven at the toy honours of such a world?

On the other hand, there was something repellent to his once ambitious soul, in the thought that such a world might seem to have the victory; and, therefore, when the first numbness had left him and the colours and sounds of things were once more coming back, he threw himself with galvanic vitality into the work that lay to his hand, and particularly into those political activities for which his gift of speech and his power of organisation fitted him.

Two months after Jenny's death, having spoken at a great meeting on some momentous question of the hour, he found himself the acknowledged leader of the Radical, rather forlorn, hope in Coalchester, and before long invitations were coming to him to help on the same hope in other towns. Never in his life — and he used often to meditate on the fact with wonder — had he been so vital, so efficient, so brilliant. His powers had acquired a firmness, an alertness, a force of influence and attraction, they had never possessed before. Of a sudden he found himself mature, a calm master of his gifts.

Yet those who sat near him at those

ZION CHAPEL

meetings might have noticed that as he sat down, pale amid plaudits, and crossed his hands upon his knees, and while his political colleagues were complimenting him to the audience on the mellow thunder of his political oratory, he was smiling furtively to himself. "It's all very funny, is n't it, Jenny?" he was saying in his heart.

Indeed it was hardly recognisable to himself as a fancy that whenever he spoke Jenny was somewhere in the audience. Sometimes a remote face might bear a chance resemblance to her, and he would humour himself with the thought that that was Jenny. For, with that self-consciousness which no modern mind can escape, he found a certain sad pleasure sometimes in noting the tricks grief played with him, loving and encouraging all its fancies — if fancies indeed they were.

When at other times he tried to think clearly, to strip himself of the illusions, as others would no doubt call them, in which he now lived, his thinking rather confirmed than dispersed them; and the more he pondered, the more he failed to realise that Jenny was dead, the surer became his consciousness that she was nearer to him (a very part of him as it were) than she had ever been in the days when others could still hear her voice and note her presence in a room. Her very death had given him a paradoxical certitude of her immortality.

Yet this recognition of her presence, on some plane of spiritual apprehension, was none the less consistent with a piercing sense of her loss on the plane where love once moved in visible beauty. That heavenly lover in him was able to give none of the comfort of its assurance to the earthly lover. That the eyes of the spirit could touch her, brought no healing to the eyes that at midnight would look up from the desk in Theophil's study to Jenny's empty chair, no touch of her to the hands that were so idle and empty now.

ZION CHAPEL

Yet there were little services these hands might still do for her. There in her own little room her own books still stood in their places. These could be taken care of, her little desk could still be kept as she had left it, with her pen laid down as she had last laid it. There were note-paper and envelopes, and ink and blotting-paper, all ready, if some day, by a miracle — who could tell? — she might steal into that room and want to leave a message. There should be fresh flowers for her to find there too if she did come.

And that new edition of Scott which was not finished issuing when she went away, she would find that complete when she came back. Her little collection of fairy books too — she was sure to glance at that! and then she would find two or three new ones there finer than any of the old ones; alas! so many beautiful books kept coming out now that she had gone.

Yet somehow she might see them, after all, if they were taken softly to that little room and laid on that table altar. When it was quite sure that no one was looking or listening, the shy soul might steal out of the air and turn the pages with a sigh.

Just so some savage lover might bring gifts of fruit and coloured beads, and bright plumed birds, to the grave of his dead love, for the future anthropologist to draw his moral of the childishness of all human idealisms.

One day, as Theophil had stolen quietly into that room on some such votive errand, an impulse had come to him to open the drawer of the desk. There might be some message for him there. Any writing of the dead we have never read before is a message.

Among various odds and ends, he came first upon one of those little tradesmen's account-books interleaved with bad blotting-paper in which the housewife writes her orders week by week.

It was full of Jenny's writing, and though the entries were merely weekly

repetitions of the same string of groceries:
— "2 lbs. of the best tea," "6 lbs. loaf sugar," "6 nutmegs," and so on, — yet, "the hand being hers," they made a record that could only be read through blinding tears; and one page which bore a severe little note, to the effect that the tea had been far from good of late, read almost like a personal revelation.

Theophil kissed the page, and, replacing the book, took up another, and his heart leapt to find it was a little diary.

He hesitated for a moment. It seemed wrong to read it, and yet he knew that Jenny's soul held nothing she would not have shared with him, and he was so hungry for a word from her though it were only a word out of the past.

The entries were not many nor long, but it smote his heart to find how large a space his name, his interests, his successes, filled there. The entries of honour were little heart-notes of evenings together especially happy; there were two birthdays still singing for joy, and sometimes there was a saying of his she had put down because it was so helpful, or a poem she had copied out; and also there were clever little criticisms of books she had read, and sometimes a wise little reflection of her own, — which brought home to him, with a certain pang, that the little child who had seemed so dependent on him had been an independent personality, after all.

As he came to the last entry, he put the book down with a gesture of pain. The last entry had been made the day after Jenny had discovered Theophil's love for Isabel. It was very brief, just a sob: "Have realised that I am no fit wife for Theophil. And yet how I love him!"

As Theophil read this, all that sad night came back to him with unbearable vividness, and he felt once more a little sobbing body crying its heart out against his. At that moment he would have endured centuries of torment just to have undone what could never be undone; and an awful thought that he had not dared allow into the daylight of his mind, suddenly sprang hideous in full view of his stricken soul: the thought that, however he might soothe its intolerable pain, he it was who had — killed Jenny. " She seems to have had a shock," a voice was saying over and over again, " she seems to have had a shock."

A shock! Yes! and Isabel, whom all this time, he had kept thrust in the outer darkness of thought, forbidding his soul to breathe her name, now sprang into vivid light again in company with that thought. In that moment he felt to hate her, and it was with a cruel mental oath he hurled her back again into the dark. It was she, *she* who had made him — kill Jenny!

But this was a thought that either must kill him, or be made endurable by some advocate of the stricken conscience; and it was with no wish to deceive himself, or to escape from his sin, that Theophil told himself that this murder of a soul, to which he pleaded guilty, was indeed no wilful act, but the accident of two tragically conditioned souls, who had planned, at their own agony, a fate of happiest life for Jenny.

Yet, the accuser urged, are not theories of life which thus jeopardise the happiness of human souls theories which it is criminal to hold? Shall you try your new ways to heaven at the risk of broken hearts?

But a voice said — was it Jenny's? — this poor Theophil and Isabel love by reason of no theory. It is yours, O ruling Fates of men, whatever you be, who must support that accusation. Theophil and Isabel loved by the compelling dispensation of the stars. They fought their destiny, and had conquered it. It was you, ye stars, not they, that killed Jenny.

And this was true: but still the little figure sobbed at Theophil's side, as again and again it would come and sob there, till Theophil's own heart broke, — that old death-crying of Jenny's broken heart.

CHAPTER XXV

JENNY'S POSTE RESTANTE

AFTER Jenny's death two letters had come for her from Isabel, who had no knowledge of what had been happening to her friends of New Zion.

There is something peculiarly sad about the letters that for a little time go on coming for the dead. Perhaps nothing more simply brings home the fact that they are no longer with us. Even little bills, circulars offering new spring goods at sale prices, come charged with pathos, and Theophil smiled at his own folly as he kept them all. Sad little *poste restante !* Will the letters ever be called for?

Theophil did not open the letters, but as days went by and no more came, he sometimes found himself taking them from their drawer and looking at them. Isabel's handwriting, though his soul would not confess it to himself, still held the power of a rune over his heart.

Had no traitor thought ever whispered deep down in the darkness of his consciousness that the way was now open to Isabel? Such thoughts indeed had come to him, but unwelcomed, involuntarily, as those foul thoughts which will sometimes torture the pure, or those base thoughts which may appal the noble.

The mind, like the body, has its foul humours, which can only be accepted with patience as a part of the inscrutable mechanism of human organisms. In moments of anger this filth and poison of the mind sometimes comes to the surface to wrong us — for it is not us, it is in truth just all that we are not.

Thus at times in Theophil's mind, that was one prayer of faithful love for Jenny, the thought of Isabel would steal, like — so his stern faithfulness pictured it — a fair devil in a church. Yet, if he opened one of those letters he knew there would ascend from it a cloud of subtle incense, which would . . . well, which he must never again breathe.

So he would replace them in their drawer, and again, some other day, take them out once more.

Perhaps, after all, it might be his duty, the mere duty of a friend, to open them. What if Isabel should be ill, should be needing him . . . should be dying!

But still the fanaticism of his sorrow conquered, and still week after week they remained unread.

Meanwhile, Isabel was living her life as she had lived it before she had heard of New Zion, with the difference of an internal sense of completion which her love had brought. Need one say that she had her hours of loneliness and longing, when she would have exchanged a thousand years of love in heaven for a touch of Theophil's hand upon earth; but these she knew how to conquer, and for most days that union of two separated hearts remained to her as real as when it had been vowed in those silent woods.

At the very moment when Jenny was dying, and Theophil had thrust Isabel away into the furthest, highest, starlight of memory, she was thinking how real their union was, how near he seemed!

CHAPTER XXVI

FURTHER CONCERNING THEOPHIL'S LIFE
AFTER THE DEATH OF JENNY

KNOWING the quick but little love
Much mention of the dead,

I hesitate further to continue that history of a grief of which, nevertheless, this book has now little heart or purpose to be other than the record, and, as what I shall write in this chapter must seem meaningless and wearisome to all but those who belong to the great Secret Society of Sorrow, it were no doubt just as well that those who have known nothing but joy should follow their natural impulse and leave it unread. I confess, too, that I should feel the more comfortable without the regard of their happy, ignorant eyes.

Sorrow is a mysticism, and to talk of it to those who have never known the initiation of tears is like talking alchemy to a child. Sorrow, too, is an aristocracy, and when Theophil came to realise that, as Jenny had been found worthy to die, he had been found worthy to suffer, it seemed to him almost vulgar only to have been happy. Happiness is such a materialist, a creature of coarse tastes and literal pleasures, a *bourgeois* who has not yet attained the rank of a soul. The influence of sorrow on the individual is much what the influence of Christianity has been upon the world. Christianity, no doubt, has robbed us of much — but then it has given us sorrow; it has taken away the sun, but it has brought us the stars. It is only in the starlight of sorrow that we become conscious of other worlds. The sun flatters our own little world with the illusion of a transitory importance; the stars show it its place in the universe, and teach it a nobler meaning for itself.

No consciousness of his gifts had ever given Theophil any such sense of his

ZION CHAPEL 239

belonging to the chosen and dedicated minority of mankind as this initiation into the Secret Society of Sorrow. He had been chosen to represent a sacred order. He stood for no lesser interests than those of Love and Death. Though he were to represent Coalchester in the House of Commons, what honour were there in that to one already so mysteriously honoured?

Tears bring a strange new sight to the eyes, and "a new perception both of grieving love" made Theophil see, and love to see, many things in the world he had never noticed before. His eyes were opened to behold the many mourners who go about the streets, the widows who walk in darkness, and all the shapes of blackness moving phantom-like through the coloured traffic; not all true children of sorrow, indeed, though wearing its habit, but, true or not, symbols of the power and majesty of death in the world. For the involuntary honour paid to death even by the ignorantly busy, and happy, he kept ever a grateful and a jealous eye; and as some funeral *cortège* passed like a dream, Charon's barge amid all the motley craft of merchandise and pleasure, he would watch sternly to see if the fat and prosperous moment would do honour to the carriages of the king. For a bowed head or a doffed hat he felt a personal gratitude. And, since Jenny died, he seemed to be always meeting that phantom procession in the streets.

Once, as he passed along the High Street, he had noticed a crowd round a dying horse. He stood with the crowd a moment, and then went on his way. In an hour's time he repassed the place, and there was the dead horse lying solitary on the side of the street; but he noted with a curious gladness that some hand had covered it reverently with a horse-cloth. "So honoured is death," he mused to himself, "that even the humblest animal on which he shall have set his seal is held sacred from the common day, and shall not be gazed upon heedlessly by the passer-by." This seemed the greatest honour he had known paid to the king!

The fascination with which from this time death and all that related to or remotely suggested it absorbed him, was, he reflected one day with a surprised recognition of the paradox, no longer the fascination of hate or dread, but almost love. Death, the arch-enemy of joy, the assassin of youth, the murderer of Jenny, — Death had robbed him of his life's one treasure, and here was he loving him, watching for his face, listening for his step, like a lover.

Surely this was the strangest of conclusions; but perhaps the explanation was very simple. Theophil loved death because Jenny had died, as he would have loved anything Jenny had chosen to do, as he would have loved life had Jenny gone on living. By dying Jenny had made death beautiful, and its gloomiest associations were but so many allusions to Jenny.

Death was to Theophil as a foreign land of which before he had only heard the name, and heard it almost without interest, as one hears listlessly of Peru. But now that Jenny had gone to Peru, the books of the world could not tell him enough about the new land where Jenny had gone, and everyone who had friends there was at once his friend, and every little dark-robed company gathered sadly to godspeed some new emigrant to its distant shore was dear to him for Jenny's sake. Besides, some of these might have heard from their friends there, might have news to tell him of the dark land. One would walk far, would listen late for such precious tidings.

Did such tidings ever come? Yes, some had even seen their loved ones again, shining strangely on the air. Why did Jenny never come like that? How he had prayed and called to her for just one sign out of the silence, one swift uplifting of the veil; but none, except that dream, had ever come. Yet one could never be sure by what common unnoticed sights and sounds the dead might fumblingly be striving to reach us in the deaf and dumb language of the dead. Perhaps it was they who led us to passages in books we had never noticed before, pointed their fingers to bright pages of faith, and left us here and there many a message of hope we never dreamed had come from them. Or might it not happen that the dead, like the living, could be unfaithful:—

> "Is death's long kiss a richer kiss
> Than mine was wont to be,
> Or have you gone to some far bliss
> And straight forgotten me?"

Perhaps Jenny already loved another in heaven, and his gift of faithfulness might some day be a burden to her . . .

This love of death was no mere morbid absorption. It was but one of the activities of a faithfulness to which the trees about the temple had become "dear as the temple's self," and his jealousy for those honours paid to death was only one expression of his eager watchfulness for the signs of human faithfulness.

Not all unrewarded was that watch. The world held some faithful hearts, — let us not ask how many, — lovers of invisible faces and voices heard no more, men and women who still shared their joys and sorrows with unseen comrades, and drank the cup of life as a sacrament of remembrance.

This sharing with the dead seemed to Theophil the essential of faithfulness, — faithfulness taking many forms, sometimes maybe misrepresentative of itself, and seldom perhaps informing its conventional externals.

A time will come in the profoundest griefs when those rituals to which young grief is so eager to vow itself will grow lifeless and conventional, the daily tasks of remembrance become as the told beads of pattered prayers. Let the worshipper

ZION CHAPEL

of relics beware lest his treasures some day turn on his hands to so much irksome lumber, and true sorrow be thus humiliated.

No! the service for the dead which is most likely to remain a vital offering of the heart is not the ceremonial sorrow of specially consecrated times and seasons, but rather the simple longing in hours of joy that *they* could have been with us. To think of our dead friends as always in their shrouds is a way of remembrance which we shall not long have heart or even interest to follow. It is only by taking them to our feasts, keeping up with them the same old human companionship, that we may hope to keep the dead as friends. A modern poet has written eight lines which were of great comfort to Theophil,—

> " You go not to the headstone
> As aforetime every day,
> And I who died, I do not chide,
> Because, dear friend, you play;

"But in your playing think of him
Who once was kind and dear,
And if you see a beauteous thing,
Just say: 'He is not here.'"

Here it seemed to Theophil was the whole duty of faithfulness. The dead know that if we remember them in our hours of joy, they are indeed remembered; and if they know anything at all, they will understand the waywardness of sad hearts better than sad hearts understand themselves.

Yet, indeed, save in the exercise of his faculties, Theophil had no joy to reproach himself with. Surely returning spring, with its terrible exuberance of warm life, was no joy. Perhaps he had looked on Jenny lying dead with less anguish than he one day beheld an apple-tree thick with blossom in the hot sun. Yes! the world had the heart to go on, to bud and build, and sing, — though Jenny was gone. And in that bright spring, see horrible and useless age still hobbling out into the beam! What was life but one huge Mephistopheles laugh beneath the windows of our dreams!

That spring James Whalley persuaded Theophil to walk with him for a week of country lanes far beyond Coalchester, letting him talk of Jenny all the time. Jenny had never been here! If only Jenny could have seen that view! Jenny had never known that flower! Did he remember those verses from James Thomson: —

"The chambers of the mansions of my heart,
In every one whereof thine image dwells,
Are black with grief eternal for thy sake.

"The inmost oratory of my soul,
Wherein thou ever dwellest quick or dead,
Is black with grief eternal for thy sake.

"I kneel beside thee and I clasp the cross,
With eyes for ever fixed upon that face,
So beautiful and dreadful in its calm.

"I kneel here patient as thou liest there;
As patient as a statue carved in stone,
Of adoration and eternal grief.

"While thou dost not awake I cannot move;
And something tells me thou wilt never wake,
And I alive feel turning into stone."

Strange joy of sad poetry for sad hearts!

Experience indeed was now divided for Theophil into what Jenny had not seen or known and into what she had seen and known; and it was one of the tricks of his grief, as time went on, to confuse the two. Sometimes he would think that Jenny had been with him at a certain place, or perhaps had read a certain book which, on taking thought, he knew she could never have seen.

Allied perhaps to this confusion was the fancy that possessed him on certain days that he caught glimpses of Jenny in little flitting figures of women about the streets. A sudden poise of the head, the way of doing the hair, a trick of walk, — just a flash and gone again; though sometimes he was haunted with more persistent resemblances, which brought him a curious mixture of joy and pain. And this perhaps is the place to record what only those acquainted with grief will understand,

and not all of those, — for grief has many contradictory fashions.

Till he had loved Jenny, women had played little or no part in Theophil's life; but with Jenny's death he found, to his surprise, that the idea of woman was strangely sweet to him. His eyes were drawn after women in the street, and he found himself longing sometimes for some woman on whose shoulder he might lean his head and weep out his grief for Jenny! He loved death because Jenny had died; was he to love women because Jenny had been a woman? Perhaps his feet had wandered in dangerous paths at this time, had it not been for the restrictions which his calling laid upon him.

These, however, did not deny him the theatre, which it had been part of his programme at New Zion to advocate, though there was seldom anything worth seeing at Coalchester Theatre Royal. Yet sometimes a good London company would call there on its provincial progress, and it chanced one day, looking into a shop window, that Theophil caught sight of a photograph of a woman that startled him with its remarkable resemblance to Jenny. It was the prima donna of a Gaiety burlesque. Such was the strange shape Jenny had for the moment taken!

For the first time after her death Theophil was at the theatre that evening. The bright lights and the music pierced him as with swords. Once more he saw that apple-tree thick with blossom in the hot sun. Yet his fancy found grim spells to lay the insolent ghost of life, and death ever at his side whispered that all this light and music and dancing was for but a little while; that those gay rouged faces, so confident in laughing beauty, and all those nimble shapes, were to the eye that had looked beyond life already stark in their coffins, with chin-cloths about their nerveless jaws. Surely the lover would trip in the shroud that was plainly to be seen from his feet to his lips!

ZION CHAPEL

Like sudden snow on a summer meadow, a white silence fell from his imagination across that fiddling, jigging, gleaming atmosphere, and everywhere the dead sat around him, watching in a trance strange antics of the grimacing dead. Curiously, in these moods, he never thought of himself as dead. Alas! life was too cruel to release him so soon to death and Jenny.

Suddenly the theatre sprang back to life again with the entrance of the prima donna. Yes, the resemblance was even greater than in the photograph. She was a little taller and more heavily built than Jenny, and it was not Jenny's voice; but for the rest, she *was* Jenny. The fascination of watching her was terrible. It seemed impossible that one form could so mockingly resemble another, and yet be so hopelessly someone else. Theophil could hardly bring himself to believe that the woman yonder with Jenny's eyes and mouth and hair had never even heard of Jenny's name. Surely, if he were to come and look into her face, she would recognise him at once, and the old common interests would rise to her lips as of old.

Theophil went again to the theatre the next night, and again the next, which was the last of the company's stay in the town; and the spell of the false Florimel grew so strong upon him that at the close of the final performance he sent up his card to the actress, and presently, as in a dream, found himself stumbling among scenery and dipping under beams on his way to the actress's room. If she were only as like Jenny close to, he felt he must follow her to the end of the world; and indeed the illusion still held as he entered the little mirrored room, smelling of powder and littered with laces and silks, — fancy little Jenny here among the grease-paints and the bouquets! It was only with the lack of recognition in the polite welcome the actress gave him that the illusion began to waver, or was it only that Jenny had forgotten him?

ZION CHAPEL

So possessed had he been with the hallucination, that he had not thought what excuse he would have to make to the actress for his visit, and it was with an embarrassing shock that the necessity of speech came to him, when he had stumbled through some mechanical words of salutation. She looked at him with a little air of bewilderment, and motioned to her attendant to leave them alone. As the door closed, Theophil had determined to tell her the simple truth.

"I have to ask your pardon," he began, "for a very strange intrusion. The reason of it is simply this. You are so like someone I love who is dead that I felt I could not rest till I had spoken to you. I trust you will excuse me, and try to understand. Yes! you are terribly like her!"

The story appealed to the actress's instinct for romance, and she entered into its spirit. Besides, the young clergyman was very interesting to look at, and the charm of sorrow was on his face.

"An actress can hardly complain," she answered, "of being taken for someone else, and though I don't know you, I feel that you have done me an honour. Am I indeed so like her? How strange it must seem to you!"

"It is very strange," said Theophil, still fascinated. Then he told this image of Jenny the story of how Jenny had died. The tears came into the actress's eyes as he talked, and it was as though Jenny shed tears for Jenny's death.

"Poor little girl!" she said; "I am so sorry for you both."

"But," she continued presently, "you should both be very happy too — for it would be worth while to suffer for so beautiful a love. . . . I feel happy," she added half gaily, "even to resemble a woman who is so wonderfully loved."

Theophil lingered on, still fascinated, till the actress suggested that he should walk with her to her hotel. Arrived there, Theophil, to the possible scandalising of Coalchester, accepted her invitation to a further chat over supper; and when at last he was back at Zion Place, his heart was aware of a new comfort and a new pain. He had leaned his head on a woman's kind shoulder, and she had let him talk and talk about Jenny; but her shoulder had been warm, and it had been sweet to be near her . . .

"A creature might forget to weep who bore
Thy comfort long " . . .

and Theophil went to sleep that night with the taste of honey upon his lips.

But with the morning there came to him remorseful misgivings, and he told himself that it had been one of the sophistries of the flesh, a call of the senses taking in vain the sacred name of Jenny; and then for his comfort he remembered how the greatest of all lovers, Dante, had craved in like manner for the solace of "a very pitiful lady, very young," and had been similarly remorseful on account of his momentary preoccupation with her.

Taking down his "Vita Nuova," he read: "*At length, by the constant sight of this lady, mine eyes began to be gladdened overmuch with her company; through which thing many times I had much unrest, and rebuked myself as a base person: also, many times I cursed the unsteadfastness of mine eyes, and said to them inwardly: 'Was not your grievous condition of weeping wont one while to make others weep? And will ye now forget this thing because a lady looketh upon you? who so looketh merely in compassion of the grief ye then showed for your own blessed lady. But what so ye can, that do ye, accursed eyes! many a time will I make you remember it! for never, till death dry you up, should ye make an end of your weeping.'*"

Moreover, Dante had married Gemma within a year of the death of Beatrice, and had even lived so scandalously meanwhile as to bring down upon him the stern reproof of his friend Guido Calvancanti; yet the world still regards him as the type of all faithful lovers. Faithfulness is an attitude of the mind, and all it touches turns to Beatrice. Yet —

> "Except by death, we must not any way
> Forget our lady who is gone from us."

CHAPTER XXVII

ISABEL CALLING

IF women were thus henceforth to influence Theophil, why might not Isabel, the woman whom Jenny had loved, be counted amongst them?

Isabel was the one woman in the whole world whom Theophil's faithfulness could not transform into Jenny. That it had been his fatal love for her that had brought Jenny to her death, his reason, except in moments of self-injustice, was robust enough to put aside.

There are excuses that we owe to ourselves, and we have a right to expect justice even from our own consciences. A sentimental conscience is the most tiresome of all altruists, and wilfully to indulge in remorse that we have not justly

ZION CHAPEL 259

incurred is to blunt our consciences for real offences. The best repentance for our sins is a clear-eyed recognition of their nature, and the temptation in some flurry of feeling to take on our shoulders the mistakes of destiny with which we chance to have been involuntarily associated, is one to be resisted in the interests of that self-knowledge which is the beginning of self-development. Before we take the scourge in hand for our own shoulders let us be quite sure that we have sinned.

There were hours, particularly those hours of sudden wakefulness in the middle of the night when our minds lose their sense of proportion, in which Theophil agonised beyond endurance, and, as on that afternoon when he had found Jenny's diary, said to himself with merciless reiteration, "She seems to have had a shock" — "It was you who killed Jenny."

These hours had to be supported as we support hours of purely physical pain. The morning brought a saner, larger view. The tragedy of Jenny's death was not to be so easily explained. In it were implicated more august responsible causes, it was part of a more general tragedy; as the original instinct to blame himself and Isabel was part of man's ancient theological habit of making man the scapegoat of the universe.

But as the thought of Isabel thus became bearable once more, it became for that very reason a thought the more faithfully to be resisted.

It might become sweet.

It was sweet!

One day the casuistry of grief brought Theophil the reflection that, as Isabel was the only woman he knew whom Jenny had known too, and that as Jenny had loved her also, she was thus destined for him even by Jenny herself. Besides, as he had realised no unfaithfulness to Jenny in his love for Isabel during Jenny's life, there could equally be no unfaithfulness now that she was dead. Moreover, if

Jenny still in some mysterious way kept watch over his life, she would understand his heart as she could never have understood it when she was alive . . .

These thoughts brought deep sorrow to him for many days, during which once more he rebuked himself as "a base person," but, curiously enough, in one who so despised the world and its opinion, it was an apparently superficial consideration that was the mainstay of his faithfulness, against these disloyal suggestions of a life that was thus reawakening in spite of himself.

There were moments when he could conceive his going to Isabel, and asking her to share his life with him; but never could he endure the thought of her bearing that name which seemed so inviolably Jenny's. Even though Jenny had come to him in a dream and asked him to give her name to Isabel, there was still the world. Though Jenny might understand, the world would think he had forgotten

Jenny. The minority of faithful hearts would grow sadder by his seeming apostasy, and the cynic would strengthen his pessimism by one more illustration of human inconstancy. The world might hear that he was loving Isabel in some Ægean isle, and still deem him faithful; for grief is allowed mistresses, but with a wife it is understood to die.

No! so long as the world lasted no other woman should steal her name from Jenny's grave.

And this was an unassailable symbol. Here the vital principle of his faithfulness was entrenched as in an impregnable fortress. He would see Isabel's heart break ere she should bear Jenny's name.

Yet while he made the vow, his love for Isabel was musical as spring within his soul, and he dared to tell himself that in God's sight he was still Isabel's as well as Jenny's.

Thus it came about that one autumn day, when Isabel's letters had lain un-

ZION CHAPEL 263

opened through spring and summer, in one sudden impulse of mere desire he had opened and read them, — not as Jenny's letters, but as messages for which he himself was hungering. He had released the incense, and as he kissed the dear writing, he momentarily forgot that it was written to Jenny, and only remembered that it had come from Isabel. In the snare of the incense he even accused himself for having left them unread so long, and then to think that nearly six months had gone by since the second letter had brought its half-playful reproach for forgetfulness. . . . "Ah! Jenny, I'm afraid you're a fickle little person, after all."

How strange it seemed to hear Jenny talked to like that — now. . . . Yes, of course, Jenny was dead. Jenny was dead . . . and Isabel was calling.

Was Jenny losing her power in this intoxicating fragrance of Isabel's words — as though for once the cross should lose its virtue in some subtle air of hellish sweetness?

O lilies from Jenny's white coffin, O little chrysanthemum that lay in her bosom, O violets from Jenny's tomb, pierce with your faithful breath this cloud of incense that is enwrapping Jenny's lover.

Alas! the power of the dead is but the power of the ideal, at once the strongest and the weakest force in the world, — a power, indeed, that prevails, but which may in some moments be shattered by the frailest whisper of the real.

Isabel was calling, and Theophil was mad to go. Come back he might, but go he must, he would. Yes! he was going.

There was only one possible way of spending that fevered night — in the train; and it was in the train, speeding on to London and to Isabel, his heart on fire, his eager eyes wasting themselves on the flying darkness, that Theophil spent it. Purposes he had none, only a desire, —

ZION CHAPEL 265

just to see Isabel again. That immediate future was too effulgent for him to think of anything beyond it.

He would see Isabel again!

From a distant starry name, withdrawn into the abysses of heaven, she would turn again to woman and a wonderful nearness.

The thought of being once again in a little room together enveloped him in a cloud of sweetness, as though the train were passing through hidden orchards.

Isabel! Isabel! don't you hear love's wings beating towards you across the night? Have you not just awakened suddenly from your first sleep in the rose-bush where you lie, and said: "Surely out there across the silent woods and meadows, where the night swallows London like a camp-fire, a train, a moving street of lighted windows, is speeding through the darkness and the dew, and in one of those little travelling rooms sits Theophil with his eyes fixed on me"?

Was it Jenny's name that Theophil was thus taking to Isabel?

No, not Jenny's name. Never Jenny's name!

He was going to look on Isabel again — that was all. Perhaps he would die with the mere joy of seeing her again — and then he would not need to think of the future. Yes! the deeps of his soul had wanted her as much as that.

It was about half-past six as he reached London; and though it was impossible to call on her for some hours yet, Theophil drove straight to Isabel's little square, shuttered and still in the early-risen London morning. His eyes chose the second storey for hers, and picked out two dainty windows as her rooms. He half expected to see the blind suddenly drawn aside and her face, a sleepy flower, bloom through the curtains.

He lingered awhile, loving each individual brick of the house with his eyes, and then, kissing his hands to the sleeping windows, he rejoined his cab, which he had left at the street corner, shy of awaking the hushed square with its clatter.

He gave Isabel till ten o'clock, which was perhaps hardly enough for a young London lady's toilette and breakfast, and then called. A pleasant housemaid answered the bell, and told him that Miss Strange was away, and was not expected till to-morrow.

Here was a surprise. He had never even thought of that possibility.

Begging leave to write Miss Strange a note, he presently found himself in Isabel's room. It was the same his eyes had blessed from the street.

So this was Isabel's room! So evidently hers, her very self!

Isabel pictures, Isabel wall-paper, Isabel chairs, Isabel cushions, Isabel desk, Isabel books, Isabel bibelots, Isabel litter, — all Isabel.

And there hung an arras portière over

a doorway to the right of the fireplace. That was her bedroom! Dare he peep in? That was her little bed. Would the housemaid catch him if he slipped in and left a kiss on her pillow? By the mirror was a grotesque little china monster with his mouth full of hat-pins. He stole one for a memory. Over a chair lay a little dressing-jacket. He took it up and kissed it.

Then he sat down to write to her. What a tidy, methodical little desk! Everything in its place. Dear, business-like, sea-witch Isabel! Here was her engagement book. He must n't begin reading her letters!

After his first disappointment, he was half-glad he would have to wait till to-morrow to see her, — for, of course, he would wait. To have thus sat in her room was almost enough for a first meeting. It was like stealing upon her while she slept.

Then he began a letter; but as he

wrote, who was this suddenly standing at his side? Was it Isabel? No . . . it was a little sobbing body quite near to his, crying as if its heart would break. . . .

Oh, Jenny, Jenny — God forgive me!

The spell was broken, the fit was over. Theophil left no letter for Isabel, and no message, and the same evening he was once more back in his little study in Zion Place, wild with remorse. O for the scourge and the fire! But what penance shall avail to ease that poor little creature's broken-hearted crying?

"She seems to have had a shock! — She seems to have had a shock!"

CHAPTER XXVIII

BACK IN ZION PLACE

THE shame of that wild unfaithfulness burned in Theophil's soul for many days. It humiliated him like a physical degradation. To have been so drunkenly untrue! It was one of those shocks to the moral nature from which it never quite recovers, and Theophil's face lost some of its steadfastness, his walk some of its firmness, for this perfidy towards Jenny.

There was only one way to make the sense of it endurable, and he threw himself into his work with a wasting vehemence. Where was his ambition? There was so much yet to do. New Zion had long since moved and hummed, and whizzed, the neighbouring towns had in a measure begun to dance to his piping, but it must be a long while yet ere his name was to London and to the world what it was already to Coalchester, — that mere microcosm of his fame.

And till London knew him as well as Coalchester, there was no real monument to Jenny. London — no longer the city of Isabel — must learn to say "Theophilus Londonderry" so naturally, that it would some day serve as an unforgettable remembrance of Jenny. He must become a great man, because a great name is the one shrine in which love's memory may escape oblivion. In the arms of his name Jenny would then be carried down the years, one woman-star saved from the night of death. Again, the world, for which in one way he had so little care, was to help him indirectly to keep his troth to Jenny.

In a sense, the mountain was already coming to this young prophet; for with the winter some of London's finest spirits were now and again to be met in that incongruous Zion Place, as visiting lecturers to New Zion. And each one, as he came, was impressed as Isabel had been on that old evening when she had discovered her colony of surprise-people. Each realised in that gravely masterful young minister a power and a force of attraction which could not long remain hidden in that little country town. Meanwhile, their visits enabled him to test his own calibre by comparison with theirs, and to realise that his instincts had not befooled him, but that he too had been called to the stage of the great world.

It was in the operation of this method of inviting the mountain that the French poet, with a reference to whom we began this history, made his fantastic appearance in Zion Place. It is to be feared that it was a conscious love of paradox that prompted an invitation from which indeed New Zion must derive the most mystical of benefits and the most imaginary of delights; but it was Theophil's whim to crown the Renaissance in Coal-

chester by this *reductio ad absurdum.*
The subtlest poetic art of France should
come in person to Coalchester, and after
days should tell that Theophilus London-
derry, while still a young country min-
ister, had bidden Paris sing her loveliest
siren-song in the musty little lecture-hall
of New Zion. It is thus power bends the
bow of the world till the ends meet, and
shoots the arrow of his name among the
stars.

With the re-awakening of his ambition,
Theophil began to realise that his work
at New Zion was nearing its end, and
that before long he must seek that larger
stage. Yet all his heart remained in
that dull little Zion Place, and while
Jenny's old mother lived he could not
conceive tearing himself away. Could he
indeed even bring himself to say good-bye
to these mean little romantic streets
along which Jenny had tripped? Could he
bear to think of the commonplace little
house which Jenny had transfigured to a

shrine being desecrated with vulgar occupation? If he could only raze it to the ground, as a cup from which a queen has drunk is shattered lest it should be soiled with usage of common lips! Some day he might have grown rich enough to buy it, and set it apart for ever, as a little house sacred to love and youth; but, meanwhile, with what ugly and noisome presences would it have been defiled!

He would stand in Jenny's room with its quiet books and flowers, and his heart would ache to think that some day harsh hands must noisily break in upon that sacred silence, and strip it of all its delicate memories. Jenny's room the lair of wild beasts, a nest of foulness and serpents! Sometimes he was thus haunted with the ghosts of those who were to riot up and down these stairs when Jenny's memory had quite died out of these walls like a fragrance of musk overborne with coarse odours.

Yes! in this perhaps are the rich most

enviable of the poor, that they can afford chapels for their memories, and their houses, thus saved from external taint from generation to generation, become temples of which the very walls breathe nobleness, whereas the very birthplace of genius itself becomes a butcher's shop; and though that genius be Shakespeare, and the old house be some day purified seventy times seven, and garnished as you please, the smell of slaughtered beasts will still cling about its rooms, and the butcher insist upon immortality too.

Jenny's old mother was soon to turn into a memory also. She had from time to time declared that she would not see another May, and had indeed on one occasion named the day on which she would die, with a curious precision, as though she had seen it written somewhere in a book, or learnt it from private or unimpeachable information. Latterly she had met Jenny twice in full daylight on the stairs, and it was evident that the old woman would soon complete that little family circle in Paradise.

But she still kept about, and whereas her old husband had grown sleepier as his end neared, she seemed to be growing more active again, fidgety and restless. She slept badly, and returned to her old habit of being first down in the morning and lighting the kitchen fire, in spite of remonstrances. Indeed, she might sometimes be heard up in the middle of the night, making herself a cup of tea in the kitchen. The kitchen had been her world, and she was already beginning to haunt it.

There it was one wintry morning they found her sitting in the old arm-chair in which her husband had died, and then they recalled her words, for she had died on the very day she had predicted.

She knew nothing of books, this quaint old woman, and had a very antiquated taste in wall-papers; yet there would seem

ZION CHAPEL 277

to be other ways of being wise, and it may indeed be held that books act too much as insulators between us and the earth, to the mysterious currents of which gnarled shapes of unlettered old men and women may be the more sensitive as lying closer to the Mother.

At all events, old Mrs. Talbot did seem to have won certain confidences from life and death refused to more consciously alert ears. Hers had been that hearing beyond listening to which secrets are sometimes revealed.

Her death was more of a loss to her son-in-law than he might have conceived, for not only was she the last of Jenny's flesh and blood, but she was the only one else in the world who missed Jenny as he missed her. Others might, through sympathy, share his sorrow, but she and he were partners in an actual loss. Something had definitely gone from each. Jenny seemed to be twice dead with the death of her mother, and Theophil's loneliness suddenly became more absolute and cut off than ever before.

There was now no one left who could involuntarily recall remembered words and traits of Jenny, and who would for their own sakes want to sit down and talk of her. All that was left that really knew Jenny was the old house itself. That remembered and talked of her still in its dumb way; and as he realised this, his mood once more changed. He forgot his aspirations toward a broader world, and felt that, not only would it be a sort of unfaithfulness to leave Zion Place, but that to do so, and to break up this familiar harmony of home, this little cosmos of friendly furniture in accustomed relations, — pictures hung so from time immemorial, rooms dedicated to this use and no other, — would be to destroy the one mirror from which could come to him still glimpses of Jenny's living face. In just that look of the rooms was the best portrait he possessed of Jenny.

ZION CHAPEL 279

Though he had always been fond of Mr. Moggridge, it had not before occurred to Theophil to make of him a companion; but about this time, as Mr. Moggridge would drop in of an evening to discuss church matters, the young minister would be surprised to note how lonely he felt when he had gone. Indeed Mr. Moggridge possessed that great undefinable gift of companionability.

What is needed in a companion is not brilliance of conversation, but the power to make you feel that you are not quite alone in the universe. Dogs and even children possess this quality for some happily constituted individuals, but for others it is a necessity that the companion be a human being.

A human being, the quieter the better, if possible a rather large man, diffusing a sense of warmth and safety, with perhaps no other gifts than kindliness and a pipe; and sometimes you have the best of company. And Mr. Moggridge, as we know, had brains too, and interesting instincts for new things. But his best gift was his humanity. Thus Theophil encouraged his evening calls and contrived to prolong them, though the two would often sit almost silent by the hour, their pipes alone making a sort of conversation.

Sometimes the young lions of "The Dawn" would come to supper, as in the old days, as Theophil called a year ago; but supper was a poor thing without Mrs. Talbot popping in and out of the room, though she had seemed comparatively unimportant then, — not to speak of eager little Jenny, — not to think of Isabel.

Yes! the sparkle had gone out of their meetings, which began to have an air of make-believe youth about them. Theophil's interest was indeed centred in the purlieus of New Zion, but it was entirely retrospective; and though outwardly New Zion was more alive than ever, it seemed to him that activity which once started goes on of itself, and he realised that in his heart he cared nothing for the work itself, but only for the music to which it had once been set in motion. Incomplete as in one sense it was, in another and more personal sense his life seemed already complete; and while in some moods he would dream of its resounding continuance, in others he would sigh that it might end.

However, for a while he would still go on living with the shadows he loved; and as he sat alone of an evening in that silent house, he would sometimes half fancy that he heard the other occupants moving about or walking overhead. That was Mrs. Talbot with a creaking basket of clean linen on the stairs, and surely that was the opening and closing of a drawer in Jenny's room. Perhaps it was only Mr. Talbot moving his chair in the kitchen.

CHAPTER XXIX

AND SUDDENLY THE LAST

HAD anyone told Theophil that in another six months he too would be a memory, and that the future to which he looked, now with a sense of new worlds to be conquered, now with a sense of weariness, was suddenly to close down on him like a dropped curtain, he would have smiled half sadly, and half proudly. No such good fortune for his sad heart! no such miscarriage of his young life!

Young life is so sure of its long lease. All about it lie the broken dreams, the unfinished projects of others; but that *its* life-work should suddenly suffer the final interruption is not to be thought of! It will die if it please of its own choosing; it will despise life and coquette with death; but to die unconsulted, with not so much

ZION CHAPEL 283

as "Will it please your honour to die tomorrow week?" is an indignity inconceivable to youth, however visionary and devoted to the worship of the dead.

Yet for quite simple reasons, as this mysterious world goes, it had been decided that Theophil was for as brief a while as possible, allowing for the leisure of natural causes, to support the life he thought he hated. Even while Jenny lived, fate, mercifully foreseeing, had willed him a brief pilgrimage; for on that night when Jenny had leaned over him with that terrible hunger of damp breath, it had been written that of that kiss Theophil should some day die.

And it was of that kiss that the following May Theophil, all his plans laid aside, engagements cancelled on every hand, eager life sudddenly trapped in this choking cul-de-sac, was dying.

Death! It was an outrage! He was young, he was powerful! He would not die!

There was May at the window. He too was full of May. He would get up and go about his work. He knew he could if they would only let him. It was the mere rebellion of unspent energies that craved to be used, like the muscular vivacity of suddenly severed limbs that still toss and twitch with hot life; yet it inspired Theophil one afternoon when he had been a fortnight or so in bed, during a brief absence of his nurse, to rise and dress, and as by a miracle keep an appointment to speak at a neighbouring town, where he had been promised for a great agitation on the Home Rule Question. Surely it was a strange enough contradiction of a year ago, when such meetings had seemed such trivialities in the thought of death. Now, when they said he was dying — had this world grown suddenly so significant that he could rise from his death-bed to make one last appearance in the paltry lists?

He spoke with an overcoat buttoned up

to his throat, and a tumbler of port wine at his side; and as the audience looked on his white hollow face, and listened to his terrible eloquence, they realised with a shudder that this was the last tragic effort of a dying man.

Alas! the great world was not to be stamped with his image and superscription, after all; and only a little faithful company of friends would know that Theophilus Londonderry was a great man.

This escapade, though it brought on death with double swiftness, brought too a calm of satisfaction which made it easier to die; and in the revulsion which it set up, life once more shrank into the background, and its little triumphs grew paltry once more. Strange, he half smiled to himself, that the man who was at last really going to Jenny should even momentarily care about doing anything else!

Yes, he was going to Jenny! So soon!

Soon he would be on the other side of that wall, soon be travelling that strange highway, on the other side of light and darkness. In a few more weeks he . . . *HE?* Would there still be *he* anywhere in the universe?

Jenny! Perhaps there had been no Jenny all these months. Perhaps Jenny stopped being Jenny forever in that last moment when she had tried to wish him good-bye. And all his daily consciousness of her presence, all the fancies of his faithful heart, had been idle as the words of a man talking in his sleep. Those little offerings he had brought to her altar, — she had never seen them; for perhaps Jenny had been an idol he had made out of air, while he had been her lonely and unheeded worshipper.

Was it really like that? and in a few more weeks would he too be as an eye that had ceased seeing, an ear that had ceased hearing for evermore?

All the wonderful colour and sound of

things! Were these waning days to be his last poor opportunities to sit at the great show?

Yes! the world was slipping like water between his hands — and he might not be going to Jenny, after all.

As these thoughts began to possess him, another thought which he had so far resisted grew more importunately pleading — the thought of Isabel. Perhaps he was going to Jenny, but surely he was leaving Isabel. Had he, he could not but ask himself, immolated a warm living heart in a fanatical devotion to a heart long since senseless and cold? Had it not, after all, been a superstitious veneration towards an ideal of faithfulness which had been Jenny's rather than his own? Had he in his heart ever ceased to love Isabel, and had he really believed that to love her too would have been unfaithfulness to Jenny?

Yes, life was nearly over, but it held the possibility still of one supreme blessedness. He might look into Isabel's eyes again.

She had but to stand by his side and his poor remnant of life would grow radiant and rounded as the most complete and blissful destiny. His heart told him that if Isabel could but once enter the room again, and stay with him to the end, however near, he would die singing the song of magnificent life.

Life is tragic, do you say? Life is cruel. Life is a splendid portico — to nothingness. Ah, no! not if in that portico you have stood for a moment, loving and beloved, by the side of Isabel. Life is splendid! life is kind! life is abounding, deep-cupped! and each minute of it is a prodigal eternity.

Thus it was that one May morning Isabel sat very still in her little room with a telegram just opened on her lap. The telegram ran: "Jenny is dead and I am dying. Theophil." And this was the first message Isabel had received from her lover since they had parted at Coalchester station eighteen months ago.

She knew nothing of Theophil's wild visit to her room, for the housemaid had forgotten to mention his call; and the strange and perhaps somewhat cruel silence could, of course, only mean one thing for her, — that Jenny had divined their love, and that for Jenny's happiness Theophil had determined that they must never see each other again.

Yet, even so, it could not have wronged Jenny for him to have sent so much in written words! Had he ceased loving her? . . . No, that she could never believe. They had *met* too really for that. And, after all, this silence was no more than their sad marriage-bond. Sad, truly, and a little tired these months had made Isabel, but they had had no power over her love. That belonged to the realities; that could never change.

"Jenny is dead, and I am dying," Isabel kept saying over to herself, divining, with love's intuition, something of Jenny's tragedy, and something of Theophil's conflict during those silent months.

"Jenny is dead, and I am dying," — a sad, a tragic message, surely! And yet, as from the first shock and consequent turmoil of that message, its real significance slowly evolved, even Isabel was perhaps surprised to find it rather a happy than an unhappy significance. Jenny was dead, and Theophil was dying; and yet, when at last she shook herself out of her reverie, her face was curiously lit with peace.

She presently discovered that there was a train north in two hours; and then she turned to her desk, and with that business-like carefulness with which we often act in a dream, she went over its contents, and methodically transferred its various accumulations to the tiny grate, which was soon blazing with unwonted summer fire. A little handful of letters she saved, and from the diminutive locked cupboard in the centre she took out a small sealed packet, which was to be included among her luggage.

All trains do not separate. There are also glad trains which bring together; and soon Isabel was in one of these, and soon it had taken her to Theophil, — to whose ears at last had come the sound of wonderful wheels in the dead street, wheels that had stopped beneath his window, a rustle of alighting, an opening and shutting of doors, an approaching whisper on the staircase, and then, with reality unutterable — Isabel.

Isabel!

You could hardly have told that Theophil was dying, and the face that Isabel thus found again was marked by none of the dreadful writing of death. His eyes were brighter, his brow more hollow, his cheeks thinner, — that was all; and he was to be of those of whom we have spoken, whose flame of life burns brightly to the end. No heavy mists of Lethe hung about his bed. Till his last heartbeat, he was to be conscious of the nearness of Isabel. For a fortnight he was thus to lie within sight and touch of her. How good life is! Think of it, a whole fortnight! How extravagantly blessed!

Isabel was living in the same house with him day after day. She was no visitor, but went in and out of the room with the step of one who is at home. If he grew weary and dozed a moment, she would still be sitting there when he awoke. She was wearing home things. One morning when she had been busied in the kitchen preparing some little delicacy for him, she had left her task for a moment to see if he needed anything; and as she had bent over him, she had worn a household apron, — a wife's apron. Yes, she was at home, she would never leave him again, never leave him — till he died.

"Oh, Isabel — to die!" he moaned one night as she sat by his side.

"But think, dear," she answered, with her head turned away, "think of Jenny."

"Perhaps there *is* no Jenny."

No Jenny! Isabel's heart gave a little cry. No Jenny! Then there could be no harm . . .

"Theophil," she said, after a silence, "have you forgotten something we said to each other that day, — something we promised?"

For answer he looked at her with awed and suddenly enlightened eyes.

"Do you mean that?" he asked. "You must n't mean that."

"Do you think I could care any more for life?" she asked. "Would you?"

"No," he answered simply.

"May I, then?"

His eyes could alone answer. He knew her love too well to affect that there would be any loss to her in the life she would thus be leaving.

"But Jenny?"

"If Jenny is there, she will understand now."

I can conceive no happier, completer moment than that which followed for these two, no more unassailable peace. If their lives were to be quite put out, they would be extinguished together; if they were to begin anew elsewhere, they would begin anew together; and meanwhile nothing that could happen could harm them, could rob them of the desire of their hearts. At the worst, they would attain their best; at the very least, they would win their most: they would die together.

To end together. It matters not how few or many years love and the beloved live their days side by side, even though their love be but the morning and the evening of one divine day, so that there be no bereaved and lonely to-morrow. The hour that takes one and not the other takes with it too all the accumulated happiness of all the years. That hour these two were to escape. Yet was there no need of haste. So long as they might, they would sit together in the sun of life. For a little longer they would say, "How wonderful life is!"—for a little longer make sure of each other.

Your eyes, Isabel! Your hair, Isabel! Your dear mouth, Isabel!

A little longer.

"Shall we go to-night?"

"Not yet . . . perhaps to-morrow, Isabel."

But Theophil was now very near death, and he might forget if he lingered on much more. Not wearily, but with music and singing must they pass through the strange gate of Death.

So at length, one June evening, Isabel made for them one last little feast,—once more wine and great grapes set out upon a little table at Theophil's bedside; and on the table, too, was the little sealed packet Isabel had taken from the cupboard in her desk.

Drawing her chair close up to his pillow, she poured out their wine, and they drank it and ate the grapes together, — no happier people in God's strange world.

As the feast neared its end, Isabel rose, and stirring the little fire into a blaze, turned out the lamps, so that the room was lit only with the light from the fire. Then she refilled their glasses with wine, and breaking the seal of the little white packet, took from it a small bottle of green crystal, the contents of which she mingled with the wine.

Then she and Theophil held up their glasses to each other.

"Let us go deeper into the wood," she said softly.

"How wonderful life has been!" said Theophil; and the two drank, with their eyes firm and sweet upon each other.

Then Isabel sat down again by Theophil's side, and leaning her head against his on the pillow, she took his hand. And the room became a heaven of silence.

Whoso would say of these two lives, "How sad!" let him consider the quality of his own happiness; and whoso would regard the life of Theophilus Londonderry as a failure, let him, too, consider the value of his own success.

www.ingramcontent.com/pod-product-compliance
Lightning Source LLC
Chambersburg PA
CBHW030748250426
43672CB00028B/1363